Unbrainwashing Yourself

How To Deprogram And Free Yourself From Brainwashing, Mind Control, Manipulation, Negative Influence, Controlling People, Cults And Propaganda

Jim Foster

Copyright 2015 by Jim Foster.

Published by Make Profits Easy LLC

Profitsdaily123@aol.com

facebook.com/MakeProfitsEasy

Table of Contents

INTRODUCTION: HOW AND WHY DOES BRAINWASHING HAPPEN?................................. 5

CHAPTER ONE: INTERPERSONAL RELATIONSHIPS 19

CHAPTER TWO: SOCIAL MEDIA 39

CHAPTER THREE: News and Entertainment Media 62

CHAPTER FOUR: RELIGION 81

CHAPTER FIVE: CULTS 100

CHAPTER SIX: EDUCATION AND ACADEMIA 119

CHAPTER SEVEN: GOVERNMENT AND POLITICS 142

CHAPTER EIGHT: MILITARY 158

CHAPTER NINE: MEDICAL INDUSTRY 169

CHAPTER TEN: CORPORATIONS.................. 187

CONCLUSION: TRUTH, LIES, AND A CULTURE OF PARANOIA 212

BIBLIOGRAPHY 228

INTRODUCTION: HOW AND WHY DOES BRAINWASHING HAPPEN?

The year was 1999. Y2K was on the horizon, and even those least susceptible to blindly falling for fear mongering news media and conspiracy theorists were sitting up to listen. Stocking up the pantry with canned goods, buying backup generators and guns, and reading survival manuals, we prepared for the unknown of the new century and the possible end of civilization as we knew it.

The Y2K bug was a software problem that derived from the abbreviation of four digit years into two digits. Programmers in the middle of the twentieth century hadn't anticipated that their code would still be in use into the next millennium. Thus, when the year 2000 arrived, it would be indistinguishable from the year 1900 and throw off the chronology of various computer programs that controlled transportation, finance, energy, and telecommunications.

Since computers ran the world, it seemed plausible that the Y2K bug would cause machines to behave erratically and money that wasn't present in the 1900 stock market to disappear. The modern world as we knew it could shut down. After all, computers didn't exist back in 1900. This was the faulty logic flying around the media in the late 1990s and coaxing the general public into a tailspin of worry and panicked spending. The news media, advertisers, retail corporations, and survivalist publications found a way to cash in on the software glitch by spreading rumors of possible Armageddon and warning people to be prepared in every possible way.

What much of the media failed to report was that the Clinton administration had begun a task force called The President's Council on Year 2000 Conversion in 1997 that was dedicated to preemptively solving all of these problems before they occurred. Experts all over the world were collaborating to make the millennial transition as smooth as possible.

Professor of Security Engineering at the University of Cambridge Computer Laboratory Ross Anderson, among other experts, said that hundreds of press reports and papers had been written assuring people that research was showing the anticipated problems to be smaller than suggested (Ross, 1999), but these were largely ignored by the media, resulting in millions of reasonable people planning for the worst unnecessarily.

January 1, 2000 passed with remarkably few glitches considering all of the media hype. Some clocks temporarily displayed incorrect dates, 150 slot machines stopped working at some Delaware racetracks (BBC News, 2000), bus tickets wouldn't validate properly in Australia (BBC News 2000), an alarm went off at a nuclear power plant in Japan (BBC News, 2000), and 154 pregnant women received the wrong test results for Down Syndrome (Wainwright, 2001).

In fact, the surprising ease of the millennial transition caused many people to shuffle out of their underground bunkers in shame and forget about the Y2K drama almost entirely. Had all of the worry and preparation and billions of dollars spent in IT services been for nothing?

On the contrary. The Y2K computer scare led to many corporations updating their computing equipment and bringing in stronger IT staff to run them. Far from merely fending off disaster, these international corporate changes led to many brick and mortar stores like Walmart and Ace Hardware sending resources into the online realm to compete with web-only startups like Amazon and Buy.com (Coates, 2000). Businesses were now ready, not only to enter into the digital age, but to take it by storm and transform the way we shop, the way we learn, and the way we think.

Welcome to the Age of Gilded Information

Over fifteen years later, it's rare that we think about Y2K and all the embarrassing things we may have believed or done in preparation, but the inertia from the questionable catastrophe has led to our being unable to imagine life without the internet. All the information in the world is literally at our fingertips. Everything from news on the Middle East to self-improvement articles to porn is accessible with a few clicks on a keyboard or the swipe of a touch screen.

Less expensive digital advancements and increasing literacy rates have made it easy for just about everyone to find the products and information they need or want. The large, expensive Macintosh from the 90s has transformed into sleek, portable, mass-marketable machines with multitudes of cheaper off-brand equivalents, all with the capacity for high-speed wireless internet connections.

People are no longer limited to mainstream news channels or the products on a store's shelf. If you want to find out more about the most recent natural disaster in Florida than the three minute news segment on the local channel provided, you can tune into another network's live online streaming. If Barnes & Noble doesn't have the book you want in the store, it's now possible to download it as an e-reader or buy it through the store's website and have it shipped directly to your home.

In fact, you don't even need to leave your bed in the morning to do some serious damage to your life savings with your debit card online. Holiday shopping has never been so streamlined.

On the other hand, these same technological advancements have also made it cheap and easy for just about everyone to produce their own information—whether it's true or not. Anyone can create a website or blog about any subject that pleases them.

In the last three decades, the freedom of speech amendment of the United States Constitution has risen to a whole new level, and the lines between fact, fiction, and outright lies have been blurred such that it's hard to tell which are the facts, which are the fictions, and which are the lies. Free speech is a beautiful thing, but it's also a dangerous and confusing thing when you think about all of the authors of blogs, ebooks, and online magazines out there who have the freedom to perpetuate pseudo science, rumors, and tantalizing but destructive ideologies.

Never in the history of time has it been so simple to pass off opinion as fact and get a hundred or a thousand or a million other people on board with it. You don't even need a degree or qualifications of any kind, though they certainly can help and be acquired for a price, sometimes not even from an accredited university or college.

All that to say that despite having all of the information in the world available at the drop of a hat and constantly competing for our attention, it's hard to differentiate between a well-meaning news article and a hard hitting exposé of Britney Spear's sudden weight gain.

With our senses being constantly assaulted with propaganda by everything from our electronic devices to our daily commute to work, many of us are easily manipulated into beliefs and purchases we never wanted and can't explain how we got suckered into, and many more of us are left with an unhealthy cynicism of all institutions from having our affections and loyalties constantly manipulated and tossed by the changing winds of public opinion what is considered to be politically and socially correct thinking and behavior.

The stars have never been closer, yet concealed so effectively.

While the digital age has opened up new avenues for mind control, brainwashing, and negative influence, it's certainly not the only culprit. Brainwashing has existed since the beginning of humanity. Whether you believe in the Garden of Eden or not, it's certainly a good metaphor for how brainwashing works:

Two humans are walking around. They see food they know is bad for them, and they start to walk away. Some snake comes by and says, "Look at how great that bad food looks. How could anything but good things happen to you if you eat it?" The humans say, "No, thank you. We don't believe you." The snake says, "I'll give you a cool car, a hot body, and lots of friends." They say okay, eat it, and die of clogged arteries years down the road.

This book will seek to address the different brainwashing tactics from our interpersonal relationships, religion, and cult followings to the military scare tactics, medical monopolies, and corporate entities.

What Is Brainwashing?

According to dictionary.com, brainwashing is "a method for systematically changing attitudes or altering beliefs, originated in totalitarian countries, especially through the use of torture, drugs, or psychological-stress techniques," or, "Indoctrination that forces people to abandon their beliefs in favor of another set of beliefs. Usually associated with military and political interrogation and religious conversion, brainwashing attempts, through prolonged stress, to break down an individual's physical and mental defenses. Brainwashing techniques range from vocal persuasion and threats to punishment, physical deprivation, mind-altering drugs, and severe physical torture."

Mind control is a process of re-education that takes away a person's autonomy over his own thoughts, beliefs, and affiliations. Think of Big Brother and the totalitarian regime from George Orwell's *1984*.

Manipulation is defined as, "skillful or artful management." In other words, a manipulator contrives ways to get a person or people to do what they want.

Propaganda is defined as, "information, ideas, or rumors deliberately spread widely to help or harm a person, group, movement, institution, nation, etc," or, "Official government communications to the public that are designed to influence opinion. The information may be true or false, but it is always carefully selected for its political effect." Propaganda not only seeks to change and reform thoughts and opinions about something, but to change and reform a person's emotions as well. Not all propaganda is necessarily bad or meant to brainwash the public into believing things that aren't true, and it's important to learn how to differentiate.

On a similar note, not all attempts at persuasion are attempts at brainwashing, which can be easy to forget.

How Does Brainwashing and Manipulation Work?

Studying brainwashing in a controlled setting is unethical and illegal due to the great potential for harm to the subjects, and as such, researchers have attempted to find patterns in brainwashing done in real life. In the late 1950s, psychologist Robert Jay Lifton studies Korean War POWs (Layton, 2006). In its most extreme versions, POWs, who were separated from their emotional support systems, underwent an assault on their identity, were made to feel guilty and associate those feelings of guilt with their own belief system, and eventually reach a breaking point of self-betrayal. At this point, brainwashers, referred to as agents, came to the "rescue" with an act of kindness and a new belief system with which to replace the old one. The agents turned from torture to kindness as the victim took on the new belief system.

There is some debate on what actually constitutes brainwashing and whether it's still brainwashing if the agent has only succeeded in changing behavior and not beliefs. Philip Graves, author of *Consumer.ology* insists that asking people what they want is not an accurate way to determine how they will act, because so many human actions derive from the unconscious mind (2010). We do things without understanding why we're doing them. Is this technically brainwashing? Perhaps not, but it's certainly a form of manipulation.

While dopamine is released when there is a violation of expectations—either positive or negative—oxytocin is the brain chemical that informs us of credibility. This is why the best lies often contain a fragment of truth that is enough to brainwash, manipulate, and control peoples' actions and thoughts.

Purpose of This Book

The purpose of this book is to bring to your attention all the dangerous ways in which the individuals, the institutions, and the media in your life are manipulating your emotions and your reason and to give you the tools to figure out reality from falsehoods. From your own personal relationships to the entities that you pay tithe and tax to, this book will remove the shiny gilded haze of the information age and give back your freedom of choice and of knowledge.

This book seeks to give you the tools to answer questions like: Is higher education really at the mercy of a liberal agenda? Is religion a social construct meant to manipulate your emotions? Do the entertainment media care about the edification of your mind and soul? Is democracy about freedom or about catering to the highest bidder?

The object of this book is not to give you all the answers, but to give you the information and tools you need to figure out the answers to these questions and more.

CHAPTER ONE: INTERPERSONAL RELATIONSHIPS

Bridgette, 22, moved to the city fresh out of college and landed her first job at a little bookstore downtown, where she met Grant. Grant seemed like a pretty chill guy. They worked efficiently together and partook of some fun shenanigans involving rearranging the cardboard cutouts of trending superheroes around the store multiple times per day and communicating from across the sales floor using a complicated series of birdcalls.

When Bridgette's long distance relationship failed after a few months in the city, Grant was there to comfort her and tell her everything would be okay. A couple of weeks passed, and he started expressing impatience with her for her continued depression, which only made her feel worse. He told her to stop thinking about her good for nothing ex boyfriend and focus on people who actually cared about her.

Bridgette feebly argued that her ex boyfriend had been a huge part of her life for several years and that it was only natural that she should grieve, but Grant shot this down.

"He doesn't deserve your grief. Do yourself a favor and move on," he told her.

Bridgette felt lucky to have a friend like Grant telling her all the things she knew her best friends back home would have said. She didn't notice when the putdowns of her ex turned into hints that Grant wanted to take their friendship to the next level. He joked about spending the night and started making a lot of sexual jokes around her.

One night, they stayed up late cuddling after watching a movie, and Grant started feeling her up. Bridgette wasn't comfortable with it and told him so.

"I just want to make you feel good," he said. "You've been through a lot."

She felt bad about her discomfort and let him continue. After all, he'd been there for her through all of her pain. Plus, she did miss having someone hold her like this.

When Grant started removing her clothing, she again protested. "I'm afraid of getting hurt again."

"I promise I'm not going to hurt you," he said. "Don't you trust me?"

"Of course," she said. But. There was a but, but she didn't know how to articulate it. Why did she feel so hesitant about this? Was she worried about ruining their friendship? She mentioned this to Grant.

"Don't be stupid," he said. "Neither of us is ready for anything too serious right now, so we'll keep being friends just like always. I promise."

The niggling fear didn't subside. "I just think it's too soon."

Grant scowled. "I think you need to let me help you forget about the scumbag. I only want what's best for you."

He had eased all of his clothes off in the space of her hesitation, and they were naked on her bed, his hands roving all over her and making her blood pound in her ears. He gazed into her eyes.

"Do you promise you won't hurt me?" she asked.

"Of course," he said.

The next morning, the deed had been done, and he was gone without a trace. She tried calling and texting him to make sure everything was okay, but he didn't respond. When she saw him at work later that day, he acted like the whole thing had never happened. He was as charming and funny as ever, but he stopped seeking out her company and asking to hang out outside of work.

Bridgette was confused. What had she done wrong? He insisted it was nothing. She tried to make it up to him by bringing him treats and making him a sweater. He accepted her gifts with enthusiasm, but refused to make time to talk to her about what had happened.

One day, she found herself at her wit's end. As she was leaving work for the day, Lynn, a coworker she'd held at arm's length for the months she'd been working there, accosted her. "Okay, girls' night," she said. "You're going to tell me about what happened with Grant."

They grabbed drinks at a bar down the block, and Bridgette told her the whole story.

When the story was finished, Lynn said, "He promised you he wouldn't hurt you. He lied to you. And now you'll do anything for him to fix whatever it is that you probably didn't do, so he's got a pretty good deal going, don't you think?"

Our Closest Friends Can Be Our Most Effective Enemies

Millions of men and women find themselves in situations like Bridgette's every day with people we care about and want to trust the most. The people closest to us—our parents, siblings, children, friends, coworkers, employers, and significant others—know us on a personal level and have access to that which can destroy us most effectively—our own emotions.

For obvious reasons, giving others access to our emotions and vulnerabilities can be a good and healthy thing. The people closest to us usually care about us most and are more likely than anyone else on the planet to have our best interests in mind. These are the people who will meet our needs, use their connections to land us that interview, and fight on our side of an argument.

On the other hand, mind control, negative influence, manipulation, and brainwashing are often the easiest to fall victim to when they come from those closest to us, whether it's a parent, a child, a friend, a coworker, a boss, or a romantic partner. Many times these people don't mean to harm us or don't realize the effects their words and actions are having on us. In these cases, initiating a conversation about the hurtful behavior will bring it to their attention in a light they may not have viewed it under, and they will want to rectify the problem.

If they refuse to see a problem with their behavior or words, then it's possible that they might be trying to manipulate you or influence your thoughts or behavior. There are several things that manipulative people have in common with each other (Ni, 2014).

They know how to detect your weaknesses and use them against you. For example, your daughter, knowing that you feel a constant sense of guilt about the fact that she grew up without a father, might use this as leverage to get you to buy her an expensive new purse. You're walking through the store. She picks up a Prada bag, puts it over her shoulder, and strikes a pose saying, "What do you think Dad would think of me now? Do you think he'd be proud?" You buy her the bag, because you want to make up for her father's absence. You want her to feel loved and beautiful. She knows this.

Manipulative people can persuade you to give up something of yours in order to serve their selfish desires. There are a variety of ways to go about this. Like in Bridgette's case, a significant other or friend might use emotional appeals in order to gain access to your body. On a similar note, threats might be just as effective. For example, they might say, "If you won't do this for me, then I'll leave you." They might also turn the tables by persuading you that the thing of yours they want you to give up for them is actually theirs. As your girlfriend, she is entitled to have sex with you. His paycheck pays the rent for this apartment, therefore he gets to say where you can put your furniture or whether you can cook tonight.

When a manipulative person succeeds in manipulating you in one way, they will repeat the exploitation until you put a stop to it. If your boss knows that telling you how reliable you always are results in you offering to take on extra work, she's going to keep doing it. If your sister knows that by complaining about how hard her life is and how little money she makes, she can get you to take her shopping and buy her things, she's going to keep complaining about her life and her income until you put your foot down and offer a different solution than taking her shopping. Maybe you suggest that she find a new job or that she try to look for the positive things in her life instead of focusing on all the negative things.

Passive aggression is another manipulative behavior that a lot of people employ as a means of either getting you to do things for them or exacting revenge of sorts on you for an annoying behavior. For example, instead of asking you if you would mind washing the dishes for her since you cooked, your mother makes a comment about how nice it would be if the dishes would clean themselves because she's tired after cooking the meal. Or instead of asking you to please remember to put the toilet seat down, your girlfriend steals the toilet paper and hides it without saying anything.

How Do I Tell If I'm Easy to Manipulate?

There are some personality traits that can make you particularly susceptible to manipulative tactics, and knowing what these are can help you to identify if and when you might be manipulated. Many of these traits are not necessarily bad, and if it weren't for the people who take undue advantage of them, they can be very positive things, but it's good to be aware that they can be abused.

If you almost always think of others and their needs instead of your own, you are likely to be very susceptible to manipulation. If you often assume that someone else's need or opinion carries more weight than yours and are used to deferring to them, this is probably something that you struggle with.

If it's important to you to avoid conflict or confrontation at all costs, then you're more likely to give in to demands just to appease people and protect yourself from having to defend your opinion or taken any blame for the fallout. After all, if you give in to someone, and their plan backfires, you can at least tell yourself that it wasn't really your fault. There's nothing wrong with wanting to keep the peace, but there's a difference between keeping the peace and having no backbone. When others perceive that you have no backbone, you've opened yourself up to manipulation and negative influence.

If you habitually try to see the best in people and give them the benefit of the doubt even when they don't deserve it, you might be easily susceptible to negative influence. Maybe you meet a man, and you really hit it off. Sure, he did make a derogatory comment about your waitress, but he pulled out your chair for you and insisted on paying for dinner. If you have a tendency to refute red flags by reminding yourself of all of the positives, then your desire to see the positive might blind you to potential negatives.

If you make a lot of your decisions based on how you think others will feel or react instead of based on what you want or know is right, then a manipulative person will have an easy time using this to his advantage. You might believe that you are being unselfish, but always giving others what they want can have the unhealthy effect of sending the message that they don't need to consider your wants or attempt to compromise.

If you are afraid of being selfish or of having others perceive you that way, you might compromise your values or needs more easily than someone who is not as concerned about seeming selfish. Maybe you feel a constant need to affirm the fact that you're not selfish, and if someone accuses you of being selfish, you will do just about anything to prove otherwise.

The following case studies provide a look at some common situations of negative interpersonal influence and manipulation that our culture oftentimes endorses, despite the harm they cause.

Sexual Coercion and the Gray Line of Consent

If asked, most people will say that rape is a bad thing. However, definitions of what constitutes rape are blurry. Is it rape if the woman who was raped was behaving in a provocative manner? What if she was wearing something slutty? What if one person was reluctant to have sex and the other kept pressing it until they agreed?

For a variety of reasons, many victims never report rape when it happens. Many sources say that around 70 percent of rapes go unreported due to shame, fear, and the reality that most of the time, the ones that are reported don't end in a conviction anyway. The many negative stereotypes about the kinds of people who get raped, as well as the fact that a majority of rapists are people the victims knew and trusted are also contributing factors to the shame and fear of admitting to victimization.

Our culture unwittingly feeds into the promotion of abusive relationships and the line between consent and coercion. Think Twilight and Fifty Shades of Grey, which grossed millions of dollars as books as well as movies and reached into the minds and hearts of millions of people.

The fact that both of these books were bestsellers and went on to become movies and find a permanent (as much as pop culture can be) fixture in conversations nationwide proves that a story does not have to be well-written, morally astute, healthy, or even very interesting in order to get so many people jumping on board with it. Is Christian Grey a sexual predator and a pervert or a total hottie and the dream man of every woman on the planet? Why is this not obvious?

Cultural Expectations of Self-Esteem and Parenting

A pervasive idea that children have fragile egos and deserve to express their feelings in any way they wish has manipulated many parents into raising selfish children who interpret "No" as "Ask me again in five minutes." The self-esteem movement took root in California schools in the 1980s and spread across the country by emphasizing the importance of high self-esteem to learning and neural development.

More recent findings have revealed that the correlation between learning and high self-esteem is actually opposite of what we thought. Children don't tend to learn more when they have high self-esteem. Self-esteem is ever fluctuating and comes from many things, among which learning is one. Self-esteem also comes from friendships, family life, and being good at things like activities or sports.

Despite the new body of evidence showing that having high self-esteem is not as predictive of success as originally thought, new methods of parenting have taken off. Many parents, afraid of damaging their children, have succumbed to gratifying to their children's every desire instantly, preventing them from having to deal with pain and failure, and treating happiness as an end-all be-all.

The Trap of "Nice" Culture

In our culture, we prize niceness. We care about not offending people, being perceived as a chill person to hang out with, and being politically correct. This sounds nice in theory, but it can lead to unhealthy conflict avoidance and the unrealistic expectation that being nice will both protect you and get you what you want.

Though our culture, as a whole, might prize niceness, not every individual sees it that way, and those who don't won't be nice to you just because you're being nice to them. In this way, tolerance and understanding of others' behavior and treatment of us can lead us to accept unhealthy, controlling relationships.

Tolerance has become something of a buzzword over the past few decades, and its meaning has transformed from a word of endurance to a word of permissiveness. While forty years ago, the word tolerance was used to denote love, honor, and respect toward someone despite your belief that they are wrong, today tolerance means acknowledging that all beliefs are equally true, which, if you think about the vast array of opposing viewpoints out there, is nice but utterly ludicrous.

When you become trapped into believing that you must blindly accept that everything everyone believes is valid and true, you open yourself up to sacrificing your own values on an altar of niceness.

Ways to Avoid and Undo Brainwashing and Manipulation

Know your rights and how you deserve to be treated by other humans. You do not deserve to have your feelings and opinions steamrollered—not even if you are wrong. A person who is trying to manipulate you will often try to make you feel like your rights are less important.

Learn how to say no confidently but diplomatically. Saying no doesn't have to seem like a personal attack on someone. If a coworker you're not romantically interested in asks you out, you are not obligated to accept simply because you feel bad for saying no. It's perfectly acceptable to thank him for the compliment, tell him you're not interested in some way, shape, or form, and wish him a nice day. Not all requests require your yes. If you can't get the extra work done at the office, someone else will have to step up to the plate.

Observe whether a person behaves in opposing extremes around different people. A person who acts like a jerk in front of his friends and like a gem while around you might be trying to manipulate you into giving him something of yours that he wants. If you notice this behavior, it may be best to avoid being around him if possible.

Learn how to hold a mirror up to a manipulator by asking probing questions. A person who is trying to use or manipulate you will often become frustrated or angry by your questions and resistance. For example, if your boyfriend keeps saying that he wants and deserves to have sex with you, you might ask him why he assumes that your body is his when he still doesn't know what your favorite movies are and why and he's made no commitment of love to you.

Use time to your advantage by saying, "I'll think about it." A manipulative person will often try to press you into an immediate answer. You don't have to give in to this ploy. Salespeople use it all the time, saying that this great deal only lasts through the day, so you'd better hop on it quickly.

Ask for second and third opinions from outside sources. One of the key parts to successfully brainwash someone is to remove him from his social circle. If you have someone in your life who demands most of your time and who makes you feel guilty about spending time with others, invite another set of eyes to witness the situation. An outsider will frequently see a situation more clearly than those within the situation will see it.

CHAPTER TWO: SOCIAL MEDIA

A few years ago, after going through a big breakup, 53 year old Jodi Buell, of Burnsville, MN was matched with a man named Claude Eichmann on eHarmony.com. Eichmann seemed practically perfect in every way. He was ruggedly handsome, well dressed, well traveled, and worked for an international mining company. They hit it off and ended up exchanging phone numbers and many phone calls. They even planned to meet in person sometime soon.

She thought she was falling in love. After all, over the last decade, online dating sites have rapidly become less stigmatized, and, in fact, considered to be a much more socially acceptable way of meeting a significant other than it was ten years ago. Pew Research Center posted an article in April of 2015 saying that half of Americans know someone who has dated or married someone they met online, and that public opinion about online dating is steadily increasing (Smith & Anderson).

Do people lie on their dating profiles? Of course, but most of them aren't any worse than adding an inch to his height or subtracting a few pound from her waistline. Statistically, most people on eHarmony and other sites like it are normal people looking for love, so it's not that difficult to understand how Buell let her guard down so quickly.

Then Eichmann asked her for money for a business venture in Ghana. She refused to send money, but she was persuaded to ship $10,000 worth of computer and phone equipment overseas along with a pair of Timberland boots and a lock of her hair. When he told her that he'd become sick and needed money for malaria medication, she urged him to contact the United States consulate. When he refused, she went to the consulate's website herself and found a link posted there about romance scams.

She said, "It was like ice went through all my veins. Everything that happened to me was listed on that website. My dream person turned into a nightmare in 15 seconds" (Shiffer, 2011). Eichmann, who was likely a scammer from an internet café in Ghana, had used Buell's longing for love and connection to manipulate money out of her, and this isn't an isolated case.

Many of these scammers are located in Nigeria, Ghana, and other West African countries and specialize in using emotional pleas and their victim's desire for love to manipulate money out of them and use them for check fraud and money laundering purposes.

Thousands of singles looking for love online have been swindled into sending large sums of money overseas to their internet sweethearts, cashing counterfeit checks, and giving out their address to have items bought with stolen credit cards sent to their house. "As far as they're concerned, this is a real relationship," Barb Sluppick, creator of the website romancescams.org, said. "They feel like they know this person. That warning just kind of goes over their heads" (Kelly, 2015).

Online dating has certainly changed our view of romance and even the progression of relationship development. Meeting potential romantic partners online does a variety of things for and against us that makes continued development of the relationship in person look drastically different than a relationship that started through a more traditional venue. For example, the fact that by the time a couple meets face to face they've already covered the usual small talk of choice for first dates, they might feel an urge to talk about more important things like political opinions or past relationships (despite the advice of numerous dating coaches who warn that these are not good first date subjects).

Hitting it off with someone you've been communicating online with can have the potentially dangerous effect of lulling you into a premature sense of security. Often, couples who meet online report that when they finally meet in person it's like their relationship has hit a fast track. Relationship milestones seem to come more quickly, and the relationship progresses at a much more rapid rate than a normal relationship would. It's not unrealistic to imagine that this is because seeing a profile of someone online tends to lay out many of their most pertinent demographics up front. You often know how tall they are, what their race is, whether they have or are interested in having children at some point, what their religious and political preferences are, and what sort of person they are looking for. Coupled with the fact that the nature of dating profiles tends to signify that the person online is single and actively looking for a relationship—or at least someone to go out with—sends two people who meet each others' requirements into a tailspin of excitement that causes them to get attached quickly.

In many cases, these whirlwind romances end in flowers, rings, and a walk down the aisle.

In many more cases, they end in delusions, heartbreak, and disappointment with the social media of online dating.

The internet with its ever-deepening pools of social media has successfully reshaped what it means to form and develop relationships in a variety of other ways as well.

Reshaping Our Relationships and Behaviors

The ways in which social media condition our minds are often subtle and unexpected. They often will creep up on us unexpectedly and take us by surprise when we become cognizant of the changes in our habits, our behaviors, and our relationships.

We expect that social media should make us feel connected to our friends and acquaintances all the time in ways that were never possible before the internet. In reality, social media provide a false sense of connectivity that, rather than drawing us closer to our peers and colleagues, actually entices us to live lives that are separated from those who we ought to be most present to.

Facebook, Twitter, Instagram, and Tumblr in all of their portable forms have made it possible for us to sit in a room with friends playing a board game while conversing with everyone but the people in the room. It allows us to feel a sense of immediacy with those who aren't physically present to us, even while they, too, sit in a room of their friends hanging out. We think that multitasking our friends in this way is maximizing our time, but we've been tricked. For even while we hold multiple conversations at once, our divided concentration diminishes the quality of all of them. We can often feel a sense of closeness that we didn't earn with those who aren't in our presence and a sense of distance that we did with those in the same room.

We expect that our social media will feed on our insatiable curiosity about other people. It allows us to see everything going on in everyone else's lives and what everyone is wearing. We can be with them vicariously, at least on the surface level. It's easy to get caught in the trap of drawing comparisons between others' lives and our own in unhealthy ways.

We are all hidden under a cloud of self-mediation. The perfect wedding might have been the perfect disaster masked by a parade of beautifully photoshopped smiles. In addition, there is a tendency, especially among the younger generations, to participate in an event with the Facebook pictures in mind. We don't savor our food, we photograph it and send it to our friends. We don't relax with a book on the beach, we take selfies of ourselves with the pigeons, book forgotten on our towel, and upload them with a sepia filter to Instagram. We've been manipulated into believing that the end result of our social interaction should be adding to the Facebook façade. This detracts from and devalues face-to-face interaction and makes real relationships seem cheap and easy, especially when most people are presenting their most trendy self.

Social profiles online give everyone the opportunity to present their best self or what they wish was their best self. On the one hand, this can be a good thing; asynchronous communication allows you to take a few minutes composing statements before you make them, a luxury that doesn't usually exist face-to-face. On the other hand, it allows people to disguise undesirable traits and blemishes that you wouldn't have missed in person. Maybe your brother's Twitter feed makes him look like a pious man who is doing a lot of meaningful things for society, but you know that in real life, he's living in your parents' basement, unemployed, and recreationally complaining about how tough he has it. In social profiles of all varieties, these discrepancies may be easy to spot for a close friend, but the rest of the world will likely never know.

Not only does social media present façades instead of people, it opens doors to viral pseudo news articles, videos, and behaviors that redefine what we talk about and attribute importance to. Maybe the factory next door is emptying carcinogenic waste into the river, but that's nothing compared with all of the media attention given to Caitlin Jenner and the transgender movement.

Social media is largely responsible for several different viral behaviors. "When the Web took off, so did viruses—and not just hard-disk-munching e-bugs. Viral behavior itself seemed to find parallels in the world the Web had wrought" (Thomas, 2007). The phenomenon known as planking involves lying facedown on objects of any variety to take a picture, sometimes with friends. You have to take a photo, or it doesn't count. "Without a photo, you're just a person lying down" (Meltzer, 2011).

It had its origins in the 1980s when a couple of kids decided to go lie down in right field during a baseball game to see if anyone noticed. Years later, one of them posted about it on Twitter and Facebook, and the game started to take off as a weird, funny thing to do.

Then, a couple of things happened within days of each other. A guy was caught planking on a police car and arrested, and another man who was planking on a balcony fell seven stories to his death. The media coverage of the events publicized planking nationwide in Australia and turned it from a few thousand people in Australia planking, to over a hundred thousand people worldwide participating in the game.

Sure, it's just a game, but the media coverage proved that it's not always a harmless game, and the fact that something as ridiculous as planking could gain so many "converts" in such a short period of time shows just how easily influenced people can be by social media. The fact that your friends are doing a certain weird activity might have been a moot point to the rest of the world before Facebook and Twitter, but now that they can document it and post it publically, it's got as good a shot as any at producing viral behavior and influencing the behavior of friends of friends of friends of friends, etc. until it's become a world movement without a cause. I mean, world hunger aside, let's hop on this planking trend and totally take the world by storm.

Social media is as effective at fueling and spreading hate and negativity as it is at spreading ridiculous international games. Curated in real time, social media like Twitter invites impulsive commentary in 120 characters or less. In some cases, this commentary has ruined careers and lives because of the thoughtless comments and insinuations that people make in posts on Twitter and Facebook. (Rudder's examples)

In June of 2015, when congress passed a law legalizing gay marriage in all 50 states, the intensity of hate speech on both sides of the issue was staggering. Social media blew up with everyone from bloggers, journalists, and averages Joes writing heated articles that, by and large, added little useful dialogue to the public discourse. People in favor of the decision flaunted their victory by telling conservatives to just get over their loss and to be happy for homosexuals. Those against the decision wrote impassioned speeches about how the Supreme Court ruling doesn't change anything in their eyes or that they should treat everyone with love. It has pretty much run the gamut of emotions, which the negative ones on both sides, at least initially, in the majority.

Social media, with its user base in the millions, is a prime opportunity for data mining, personalized marketing ploys, psychological study, and experimentation.

Marketers know that you've been looking at parenting books on Amazon, and they can present you with personalized advertisements on your Facebook home page for nursing bras and baby wipes. The gurus who work for Facebook will say that the advertising is what keeps the site free for everyone to use, but though we don't pay money for it, we still pay for it in other ways. Time is the obvious currency. The less obvious currency is the barrage of constant appeals to our emotions and pocketbooks, which can cause us to experience willpower depletion more quickly than if we hadn't gone on social media at all.

Depletion of our willpower happens when we are asked to make a constant stream of choices. These may be as simple as saying no to the ad selling dresses for crazy low prices, but it's still a decision that we make not to do or buy something, and it contributes to the fatigue that we feel from making too many decisions in a day.

Was the gay pride rainbow filter offered by Facebook to show support of the LGBT community simply that, or is it another opportunity for data mining and future experimentation without the consent of its users? Right now, Facebook is claiming that,

"This was not an experiment or test, but rather something that enables people to show their support of the LGBT community on Facebook. The point of this tool is not to get information about people" (Roark, 2015). But the fact that Facebook has admitted to doing data mining and psychological experimentation in the past leaves us skeptical that they won't do it again. The rainbow filter might not have plans at this very moment, but they now have the data, and no one is saying that they won't use it somehow in the future.

Marketing through social media and online games reaches a more disturbing level when the marketing is aimed at children, who don't yet understand what marketing means. Spokes-characters have been used to develop "personal" relationships with children while playing games online for the purpose of making them more susceptible to marketing ploys. Because children come to view these characters as celebrities, they have a lot of psychological pull on what children will believe and what products they will want to buy (Thomas, 2007→page 19). Fairy tale characters are frequently hijacked and used as corporate spokespeople, because children know and recognize them, and as such, they believe in them and their message, even if their message is to buy things.

"Like real genetic material, these [ideological codes] infiltrate the way we do business, educate ourselves, interact with one another—even the way we perceive reality," says Douglass Rushkoff in his paper entitled *Media Virus! Hidden Agendas in Popular Culture*. Our sensibilities have been manipulated.

Signs That Social Media Has Brainwashed You

A reasonable argument can be made that what social media does to us isn't actually brainwashing us, but when you think about it, it has followed many of the requisite steps of traditional brainwashing, even though they look different.

Social media is successful in separating us from our support systems by causing us to replace our face to face time with online time. We feel like we are still close with our friends, even while we spend less time actually with them. Through viral news and a constant stream of opinions on various topics, especially combined with the cultural ideology that we should treat every opinion as truth, our own beliefs can sometimes be lost under the mountain of others and the pressure to treat all things equal, even if they're not. When we feel sufficiently depleted from an excess of social media use, someone is always ready to sweep in, let us know that it's okay, and offer us a new perspective or behavior with which to replace our old ones.

If you remember the definitions of brainwashing from the introduction, "brainwashing attempts, through prolonged stress, to break down an individual's physical and mental defenses." Social media, through prolonged exposure can break down our defenses by depleting our willpower such that it's more difficult to resist making poor choices, taking us away from our real life relationships, and wounding us with an onslaught of media propaganda telling us so many different things about what we should be thinking and doing that we're tired and confused. Our defenses are down. We think, "Yes, let's plank on the train tracks."

The following are signs that social media has or is in the process of altering your neural pathways and causing you to think in ways that you never meant to think.

Despite active participation in social media, you feel lonelier than ever or have a hard time taking interest in friends and family outside of social media. Do you pressure your friends to join Facebook so that you can share photos back and forth with each other?

You obsessively check social media or think about it when you are not on it. If you feel a knowing or itchy feeling that you can't go a few hours without checking on what's happing in the online world, your media may have you in its manipulative phone-sized clutches.

You are never satisfied with the person or people you are with because of a burning desire to figure out if there's someone better out there you could be spending time with. Opportunity cost is always something to be aware of—if I do this thing, I can't be doing that thing—but if you're reversing the concept such that you feel bad about the time you spend with people in person when there's a huge world out there that you can see on your phone—and shouldn't you, like an alien life form, be trying to make contact with what's out there?

You spend significant portions of your time un-ironically taking selfies with duck lips and you fully believe that this is a great strategy to make you look hot and desirable.

You spend hours scanning newsfeeds looking for interesting photos or articles to click on. This can become an addicting habit. Pretty soon, you're not even consciously looking for anything, but scrolling down the feed mindlessly staring at your screen. You don't wonder why everyone is saying the same boring stuff today that they said yesterday. You don't wonder if you should be doing something else right now. Anything would be better than the zombie scroll down the Facebook or Twitter feed. It's interesting that they call it a feed, though in a way, it is a feed. It feeds you zero calorie, zero nutrition pseudo food that causes you to forget about the stack of books on your bookshelf that you bought before you signed up for Facebook and haven't made time to read yet.

You go to your favorite social media gurus for answers on everything from relationship advice to home decorating. Historically, advice was asked for and given by close friends and family members in your immediate social circle. Now a question can be posted on Facebook and receive responses from whoever is on. This isn't necessarily a bad thing, but it you're consulting strangers about how you should live your life more frequently than you're consulting the people who know and love you, that might be a sign that you put too much weight on social media to be there for you and solve your problems.

The advertisements on the side of your Facebook page seem like they might know you personally and be stalking you. How did the powers that be at the Facebook corporation know that I wear size 8 shoes, that I am insanely into green polka dotted purses right now, and that I'm going to medical school, though not on a Ph.D. program but a D.O. program? The quick answer to this question is, simply put, data mining. You use Facebook, and it uses you.

Tactics To Overcome Social Media Brainwashing

Unplug from your social media for a while. This might come as a shocker to you, but it won't miss you while you're away. The friends whose wedding photos you won't see if you log off aren't going to be any more offended that you missed out on seeing photos from their big day than they were that you didn't go to the live wedding in the first place.

Pay attention to the people you're with by focusing on the unmediated present. The cliché goes, "There's no time like the present." It might be more accurate if it said something more like, "There's no time *but* the present." If you spend your present in a continual state of ignoring those in the room with you in favor of those available through your phone, then you are not making the most of your senses and your time on earth. To use another cliché, life is too short to replace coffee dates with Skype chats.

Learn how to ask probing questions about the news and advertising you are presented with. What is the agenda? What is it masking? What do I have to lose by giving over pieces of myself to the worldwide public? A person who has taken time to reflect on the reasons for his beliefs won't be easily blown and tossed by the media current.

Become cognizant of the time you spend on social media. Do you spend several hours a day browsing your Facebook or Twitter feed? Does that time cut into time you could be spending developing real relationships with people face to face? Don't let Facebook feed your soul. It would be like eating fruit rollups for every meal. It's tasty and fun for the first few meals, but it produces diminishing returns in happiness and health if you continue to consume it for most meals indefinitely.

When it comes to social media, an important question to keep asking yourself on a regular basis is are you using it, or is it using you?

CHAPTER THREE: News and Entertainment Media

The term "Yellow Journalism" is shortened from "Yellow Kid Journalism" after the popular Yellow Kid comic by Richard F. Outcault at the end of the nineteenth century. The Yellow Kid was a bald snaggle-toothed kid in an oversized yellow nightgown who stereotyped the very poor in New York City. Sometimes making fun of the poor and sometimes making fun of the rich, the Yellow Kid became a popular and humorous political figure of the time.

Outcault was working for Joseph Pulitzer at the *World* when William Randolph Hearst lured him away with a large salary in order to increase his paper sales among those whose loyalties lay with the Yellow Kid. Pulitzer hired another cartoonist and created a second Yellow Kid, and the two Yellow Kids battled each other through the remainder of the century.

The line between news and entertainment has become blurry as Pulitzer and Hearst competed for the highest newspaper circulation in New York City in the 1890s. Sensationalized news stories became a norm, because they drove up newspaper sales and kept Americans hungry for more exciting stories. Often, news was altered to fit the story ideas that the editors thought would sell the most papers. Sometimes, stories were fabricated and interviews were faked. Pictures would be added to simply create dramatic appeal and make interesting insinuations.

Pulitzer and Hearst were not overly concerned with what was true, but with what would drive circulation higher than the other's.

For example, when the Spanish-American War was on the horizon Hearst saw it as an opportunity to increase his sales and promote his own reputation. He paid correspondents to station themselves in Cuba and come up with stories of violence and brutality, so that he could entice and sway public opinion in favor of the war. The correspondents reported back saying that there wasn't anything happening, and there didn't seem to be a war. In a famous telegram, Hearst reportedly said, "You furnish the pictures and I'll furnish the war."

So, they wrote stories about executions, female prisoners, starving children, and brave rebels to effectively inflame public passions about the war (PBS, 1999). When the battleship, USS *Maine*, sank in the Havana Harbor, the *Journal* pointed a finger at the Spanish, despite a total lack of evidence that they had anything to do with it, saying that they had put a torpedo under it to blow it up. As readers jumped on board with the war, the president was effectively pressured into sending troops to Cuba to fight the Spanish. This was, arguably, the first war that the news media had such a pivotal role in causing.

Eventually, the outrageous, often untrue, news accounts that each paper printed started to hurt both of them. Pulitzer became plagued with guilt about his yellow journalism and sought to turn the *New York World* into a respectable publication again, while Hearst tried to get nominated to run for president and failed after stories printed in his own paper caused the public to speculate that he might be suggesting the assassination of President McKinley.

While most news media today is held to higher standards of ethical reporting, that doesn't mean that it's less influential, or that a newspaper or TV station isn't concerned with circulation, viewership, and money. News media today still have the same biases and the same propensity to sensationalize what they can get away with in order to drive sales, but they must be a lot more subtle about it today.

Setting an Agenda of Fear

Around the time that the Watergate scandal started to break, journalism professors, Maxwell McCombs and Donald Shaw, were coming up with a new theory of how the news media shapes our perspectives. They called it Agenda Setting Theory. The idea is that the news media determine what news events we are exposed to and therefore what we think and talk about. "The press may not be successful much of the time in telling people what to think, but it is stunningly successful in telling its readers what to think about," said political scientist Bernard Cohen (1963).

They went on to find that every news source has its own bias, even the ones that claim otherwise. *Newshour with Jim Lehrer* might take a fairly moderate view on most things, but the slightly more liberal bias and framing might be enough to sway opinions on the edge more in favor of a liberal idea than a conservative one. That being the case, the news media subtly inform our opinions about different events by framing stories in a specific way. While some media sources will make a school shooting about race and ethnicity, others will make it about violent video game use or the deficits of the educational system. Depending on which newspaper you read or program you watch, you might unconsciously find yourself assuming the subtle (or not) viewpoint of the source from which you read about the event.

The news media can make some topics more salient than others by giving them more words and featuring them more prominently than others. We take our cues about what's important in the world from what story has the most words on the front page of the paper and what the news anchors spent the most time talking about.

On the flip side, news media can make other topics less salient by saying less about them and burying them in the back pages of the paper or only mentioning them in passing on the evening news.

In addition to Agenda Setting Theory, another theory related to news and entertainment media, particularly network television, was making its way onto the scene in the 1960s. Researchers George Gerbner and Larry Gross developed the theory out of an interest in seeing what long-term effects heavy television watching was having on people. Interested particularly in what TV violence does to a person's perspective over time, they devised a method to figure out the amount of violence present in each primetime show and then invited light and heavy television viewers to take a series of surveys that test for the shows they watch, how much time they spend watching television, and what their worldviews are like.

Gerbner predicted that, due to the quantity of violent television programming people digested every day, they would believe that the world is a meaner, scarier place than those who rarely watched TV (Griffin, 2012). Decades of research revealed that he was correct. Moreover, further analysis of his studies revealed that not only to people who watch more violent television believe that the world is worse than those who don't, but the content of the program itself influence who people believe the violence is most likely to happen to.

His studies repeatedly found that violence on TV was more likely to happen to minority groups, children, the elderly, and women than to young and middle aged Caucasian adults. Because of this, people who view more violent television have a much greater likelihood of believing that violence usually happens to minorities. For example, if you are an elderly African American woman who watches a lot of TV, you will experience more fear that something violent is going to happen to you than a 35 year old white male will, whether he watches a lot of TV or not. The percentage of people who fear violent crimes happening to them is actually much greater than the percentage of people who experience violent crimes.

The current body of cultivation research suggests that there is very good reason to believe that TV has a huge impact on the way people think and feel about the world and about themselves.

Fear Mongering and Creating Public Enemies

Perhaps the news has come a long way in ethical reporting since the days of Pulitzer and Hearst and yellow journalism, but the fact remains that people still like to be intrigued and surprised by a story. That being the case, news outlets seek to dig up interesting stories and put a slant on it that, while not necessarily false, creates public alarm that is not quite warranted.

Before September 11, 2001 created enough interest to fill newspapers and programs for the next several years, the news media turned sharks into public enemy number one in the slow news season of the summer of 2001. In a CBS News article published 4 days before September 11th, the hot topic of the day was whether the government was to blame for the multiple cases of shark attacks that had been publicized throughout the summer (CBSNews.com Staff, 2001).

One proponent of this idea, Sean Paige of the Competitive Enterprise Institute, claimed that cases of shark attacks had been rising since the government placed restrictions on shark hunting in 1993. No experts in the field of marine biology or ichthyology were able to back up this claim, causing one to suspect that it's not the number of shark attacks that had risen, but the amount of media coverage of them.

Ocean conservancy advocate, Sonja Fordham, argued that, "It's a play on public fear to further [the] economic agenda [of those who are frustrated by the ban on shark hunting]." And who knows how many people were persuaded not to visit the ocean on vacation because of the overwrought shark attack publicity?

Similar public enemies that have been blown out of proportion in order to create a sensation in recent years are the killer bees, Avian Flu, Anthrax, the Ebola virus, a flu vaccine shortage, and that terrorists are coming to kill us all. If there's one thing that the news media excel at, it's getting us to fear for our lives whether there's a very good reason for it or not.

The Shoe Doesn't Fit: Beauty Ideals In Advertising and Entertainment

Violence isn't the only way TV programming and movies cultivate our perspective of the world. In addition to violence, the TV industry has hijacked our opinions in other ways by perpetuating beauty ideals that are unrealistic and have ruined the lives of thousands of men and women. Certain body types have been given more positive press than others, which has fed into a culture of negative body image, eating disorders, and plastic surgery.

In her book called *Deadly Persuasion*, Jean Kilbourne explores the ways in which mass entertainment and advertising subvert a healthy view of oneself, specifically focusing on feminine thinness and beauty ideals and how advertising affects them. She says, "Mass communication has made possible a kind of national peer pressure that erodes private and individual values and standards, as well as community standards" (1999). She goes on to say that even girls with loving, supportive parents are more frequently trading their identities for those of advertising supermodels and engaging in risky behaviors and addictions so that others will perceive them as sexy and desirable. Perhaps unintentionally, the media have propagated the myth that good things happen to beautiful people and bad things happen to the ugly and marginalized.

In a study by Kristen Harrison, which followed the framework established by Gerbner, 36 popular TV shows were evaluated based on the main female character's body type. By using Gerbner's process of rating shows based on how thin the main characters in television shows are, Harrison was able to determine both that the female characters in almost all of the popular shows fit with the culturally mandated thin ideal of a 36 inch bust, 36 inch hips, and a 24 inch waist (2003). This is an impossible figure for the average woman, as losing weight at the waist and hips usually causes a decrease in breast fat as well.

Furthermore, Harrison found that 69 percent of female characters in popular TV are thin or underweight (2003), 13 percent of characters are overweight (Levine & Harrison, 2009), and over half of American women are overweight. This disconnect between what women are covertly told they should look like and what they actually look like creates greater dissatisfaction among women who spent more time watching these shows. They had a view of female beauty that was most in line with that of the shows they watched and were more likely to be dissatisfied with their own bodies and the way they looked.

Additionally, Kilbourne says that "about 70 percent of college women say they feel worse about their own looks after reading women's magazines," which leads to what other researchers in the field call self-objectification. Self-objectification happens when women come to view themselves in terms of what they look like rather than who they are as people.

Most of the time, the main character in the show is the beautiful woman who is able to overcome all of her challenges in the end and win the stud muffin from the mean girl. Conversely, overweight women "are significantly less likely to be portrayed as attractive and to be judged attractive or desirable by other characters" in the show (Levine & Harrison, 2009). This sends a subtle, but clear message to women that beauty is not only objective but a means of getting what you want out of your life.

The Truth About Programming

As the middle class in America grew, and luxury became more affordable, mass entertainment appeared in living rooms across the nation in the form of radio and television. For the first time since the printing press, there were attractive new ways to market ideas to the masses.

While the television and radio programming in and of itself has drastically changed the ways in which we view the world, the programming itself is only a fraction of the picture.

Programming is paid for by advertisers, who recognize news and entertainment as vehicles to get word about their products and services into the minds of the public. In order to win better sponsorship, networks produce programming that will most appeal to the advertisers' target audience. Higher viewership of a certain show means continued sponsorship and more money. This is why excellent shows with smaller, though very loyal, fan bases like *Firefly* and *Pushing Daisies* were canceled in the first season, to be replaced by shows that seemed like they should fit a more financially lucrative demographic.

Thus, news and entertainment programs alike are not about bringing truth and art to the masses or even about making you laugh, but about getting you to sit through the almost fifteen minutes of advertising that play for every hour of programming on TV.

Advertising is the basis for radio and TV programming, but it doesn't end there. Ads invade our Google searches, our social media, our videos, and even the movies that play on the big screen. In any given film, a character might be drinking a Coke, using an Apple computer, watching TV on a Sony, and mixing a bottle of Similac baby formula, sending us the subtle message that these are brands and products that our favorite characters endorse—and we should too.

This phenomenon is not limited to adults with the ability to logically deduce that they don't need to drink Coke in order to win the girl or be skinny to be loved. Children's programming is rife with examples of creating brand loyalty in children that will last a lifetime and bring companies millions in revenue ten and fifteen years down the road.

Deprogramming Weapons of Mass Media

When you are presented with an unbelievable news story, check multiple sources of varying political agendas. Don't assume that once you've read one you've read them all, as you'll never be able to escape bias entirely. Even the most moderate sources overall will slant one way or another on individual stories. After all, a story with no angle is a boring story indeed.

Be vigilant about the television programming and movies that you watch. If the shows you like to watch are violent or overtly sexual in a way that portrays people inaccurately, it would be wise to limit how much you watch. Several hours of TV viewing every day will greatly affect the way you view the world and other people.

Be aware that the purpose of your favorite shows is not to entertain you but to persuade you to buy things. This warning is not made so that you derive less enjoyment from your favorite programming. Au contraire. It is made to remind you that the corporate entities paying to keep your favorite show on the air are doing so only for the opportunity to get you to buy stuff from them. Consciousness about the purpose of TV and advertising will keep you grounded and less susceptible to manipulation.

Another thing to be aware of is that TV conditions you to passively accept what is presented to you. Unlike playing family board games or reading a book, watching TV requires nothing from you mentally. You don't have to read or respond to what's going on. It does all the work for you, so all you have to do is follow the leader. As a result, it's easy for TV to keep us locked in its digital embrace blindly accepting the politics, the ideologies, and the lifestyles that it feeds us. The simple solution is to watch less

TV and instead partake in activities the effects of which you have a greater level of control over.

The more difficult solution is to practice watching TV and reading the news in a more active manner. What does this mean? It means observing what's actually going on in the show. It means asking questions. Which characters are good and which are evil? Is this in line with current stereotypes? What do I think about this? Is it right or wrong? What is the meaning? What would my friends or family think about this? If you are watching with a group of people, engage in discussion over what has happened in the show. Say what you liked and didn't like and why. Try to step back and objectively ask if the story was successful.

The point of mass media is to manipulate your opinions so that corporate entities can make money, but that's not to say that you have to let that be the only point. The best weapon against mass media's pull is a developed mind that knows how to ask good questions.

CHAPTER FOUR: RELIGION

Religious fear and zeal has fueled and manipulated human thought and actions for thousands of years, and not even science has been able to abolish rampant fear of the supernatural from the back burners, and in many instances the front burners, of public discourse. The *Harry Potter* series may have given witchcraft some good PR in the developed world, but modern day fear of witchcraft and associated hate crimes persist. In some parts of the world, witch trials, hangings, burnings, and torture are every bit as prevalent as they were during the American Salem Witch Trials of the 1690s.

A Gallup poll taken in 2005 revealed that 13 percent of people from Canada and the United Kingdom reported believing in witches, while 21 percent of Americans reported the same (Lyons, 2005). Type "witchcraft" into Google, and hundreds of websites pop up about everything from identifying witches and witchcraft today to using witchcraft to control people to witchcraft accusations in current events.

One such recent article mentions that the family of an 8-year-old girl from London accused her of being a witch and attempted to "beat the devil out of her" by abusing her and rubbing chili peppers in her eyes. While London officials were able to rescue her from the situation and prosecute three of her family members, officials in other parts of the world are just as guilty as the people they have authority over at spreading a cultural fear of witches.

In developing nations, where fear of witches is even more of a norm, accusations of witchcraft have led to a lot of violence and injustice.

In Zambia, where 25 percent of pregnant women are infected with HIV or AIDS, men, women, and children are accused of causing it through witchcraft. They are frequently hunted and killed using a poisonous tea (Schons, 2011).

In Nigeria in the 1970s, a few people became extremely wealthy in the oil boom, and this sudden turn of good luck was seen as a sign of witchcraft. Nigerian children accused of witchcraft have been burned and poisoned as recently as 2007.

Albino people are killed as ritual sacrifices in Tanzania, because community witch doctors have persuaded people that albinos' skin and body parts are magical and bring good luck.

In India, the neighbors of a female landowner, who is usually an old widow, will sometimes accuse her of witchcraft. Fearing what will happen to her if she remains, the woman will often flee her home, and the neighbors will be able to take her land for themselves. In these instances, the cultural belief in and fear of witchcraft is used as a crutch for the neighbors for the purpose of obtaining the land. The ones making the accusations don't so much fear that she is a witch, but they know that accusing her will incite fear in other community members. Fearing what those who fear her will do to her at the suggestion of her neighbors, she has no choice but to run away.

Fear of witchcraft has also had a hand in the rampant Ebola spread in Sierra Leone and other parts of Africa. Many villagers and their leaders, believing that the medical doctors bringing relief were responsible for causing the virus through witchcraft, used violent means to keep the doctors out of their infected villages. According to a *Telegraph* interview with Benjamin Black, even those who show up at the treatment centers with symptoms resist treatment, because they believe that their symptoms must be from witchcraft rather than from the Ebola virus (Freeman, 2014).

Adding to their fear, when they arrive, they often see doctors injecting the sick with needles in hopes of curing them. Since most of these patients are receiving the medicine too late, they die, and the villagers who witness this jump to the conclusion that the doctors are giving their people a lethal injection instead of trying to cure them.

Though 90 percent of people who contract Ebola die, those who live to return to their villages risk the stigma associated with having had Ebola. Sometimes, family members refuse to accept them back out of fear that they are still dangerous. While efforts are being made to educate the public about disease, as well as to assimilate recovered patients back into their societies, superstitions are not easy to overcome.

A Common Scapegoat

Religion has claimed a hefty amount of blame for brainwashing, mind control, manipulation, negative influence, and propaganda over the last thousand years. From the Christian crusaders of 1095 to the Muslim suicide bombers of today, the dark side of religious extremism has been exposed time and again. But while it's easy to assume that organized religion is at fault, it's more difficult to look beyond the religion and see what else lies behind the brainwashing and manipulation and whether the religion itself is truly at fault.

Religion in and of itself does not largely exist to persuade people to do what they shouldn't, but rather the opposite. When acts of violence and oppression are committed in the name of a certain religion, it's important to look at the possible ulterior motives behind the violence. Does the Christian faith say to judge your neighbor and heap burning coals of guilt on his head for his ungodly ways? In fact, it says quite the opposite, and you can be sure that when a Christian (or a Muslim or a Jew) is acting in opposition to the tenets of his faith, there's an agenda being served that has little to do with his faith or God's will and a lot to do with a social or political agenda he will personally gain from for pushing.

Many such brainwashing myths are associated with the main world religions, which will be explored in the following sections of this chapter.

Atheism: Not a Religion?

In the sense that atheism takes a stance both on the presence of a divine figure and the existence of an afterlife (that stance being that neither exist), atheism could be considered a religion. Pippa Evans and Sanderson Jones, cofounders of the atheist church in London, insist that atheism is not a religion in a *New York Times* debate piece from 2013. The irony is that their attendees do all of the things that churchgoers do—sing together, listen to speakers, have quiet contemplation, and get to know the other people attending. "Church has got so many awesome things going for it," they admit.

Most atheists will probably say that atheism is not a religion. The interesting thing is how impassioned some of those who are (arguably) brainwashed by Richard Dawkins's *The God Delusion* and other pop culture bestsellers can become about there being no higher power, no life after death, and no higher meaning to what they are doing and saying.

For not being a religion, atheism definitely has some religion-like passions.

Buddhism: Must Doubts Be Buried?

Tantric scriptures do not require that a Buddhist bury his doubts about his leader, referred to as a guru, or his faith, yet many Buddhist monks choose to bury these doubts anyway. They believe that any doubt they experience might jeopardize their shot at enlightenment.

Says Stephen Schettini, author of *The Novice*, "The question that most guru devotees avoid at all costs is the one that mindfulness poses most insistently: Is your view of the guru an example of heightened perception, or the projection of an ideal? When I could no longer isolate these two perspectives from each other, I lost my tantric faith and migrated to the lesser vehicle. It was a step up to reality at the cost of great hand-wringing, guilt and self-doubt" (2012).

There are different vehicles of Buddhist faith, and doubt regarding the guru simply removes one to a lower vehicle. Tantric faith requires faith that the guru is in every way enlightened. The reality is that the guru is human and makes mistakes. The brainwashing happens when the monk seeking enlightenment choose to ignore this reality and believe that he is infallible.

Christianity: Divorced from Science?

Christianity is frequently accused of being a faith that brainwashes its followers with stories that defy science. Despite archaeological evidence to the contrary, many Christians hold that the earth must be as young as a few thousand years old and that evolution is incompatible with what the Bible teaches. Because of this seeming incongruity many Christians either decide to eschew their faith in favor of the tangible evidence or to cling blindly to their faith, because rejecting it or examining it are both too distasteful to them.

But do science and the Christian faith truly contradict each other? The Bible, after all, was not written as a scientific treatise about how atoms and molecules move and react and how DNA forms. It's a religious text, the point of which is to inform us that God created the earth, not to give a dissertation on why he decided that electrons should have a negative charge.

In fact, Christian scientists argue that scientific evidence enriches their faith, not enshrouds it. They say that when Genesis describes the earth as formless and void before creation, it could very well be because no intelligent life had yet evolved. Many Christians would agree that it is clear that God created the world scientifically and then gave us the gift of discovering it for ourselves.

Hinduism: Accept All Religions?

Hindu thinker, Dilip Mehta, asks whether Hindu people are deluding themselves by claiming that their religion says to accept all religions. He says that, logically, this cannot happen, because many religions, particularly the Abrahamic religions (Christianity, Judaism, Islam) are exclusive religions that don't share the same accept all religions philosophy. To accept Christianity is to reject Hinduism. The same goes for Judaism or Islam.

Logically then, Hindus can only accept other religions that also accept all other religions. He goes on to say that, similarly, Hinduism is not primarily a religion of love and nonviolence, because there are examples of violence happening all over sacred Hindu text.

He says, "Hinduism never said to tolerate nonsense. When 60,000 sons of Sagar tried to play with Kapil Muni they were immediately burnt to death. When Shishupal started abusing Shri Krishna, he was given limit. When he crossed the limit of 100 abuses he was killed even it was only verbal abuse. Attack on Dharma or on sages was never tolerated" (Mehta).

Islam: A Religion of Jihad?

The short answer to this question is yes. But the word Jihad is commonly misunderstood and misinterpreted by Muslims and the rest of the world. Many of us tend to assume that it means holy war, but the Arabic word is more literally translated to mean striving or struggling. This struggle isn't necessarily an external, political struggle, but can also be an internal struggle of a Muslim follower or an external striving to share the Muslim faith with others.

If military jihad is necessary, then there are certain rules governing it. "If military jihad is required to protect the faith against others, it can be performed using anything from legal, diplomatic and economic to political means. If there is no peaceful alternative, Islam also allows the use of force, but there are strict rules of engagement. Innocents - such as women, children, or invalids - must never be harmed, and any peaceful overtures from the enemy must be accepted," says the Islamic Supreme Council of America.

The council goes on to explain that a military jihad is not something that anyone in the religion can declare. It must be declared by a certain authority figure, studied extensively, and judged to be absolutely necessary to protecting the religion. Moreover, a jihad is not meant to be a war waged on other religions. The Islamic Supreme Council of America puts it like this: "The Koran specifically refers to Jews and Christians as "people of the book" who should be protected and respected. All three faiths worship the same God."

Judaism: All or Nothing?

It doesn't come as a shock that there are a lot of rules and laws and commandments in the Jewish faith. Read the Torah, and you'll find that it's packed full of them. There are rules concerning what one is allowed to eat and drink, what chores one isn't allowed to do on which days, how long a beard must be, what constitutes clean and unclean objects and actions and what the procedure is for becoming clean after making oneself unclean. A lot of these rules are no longer practiced, but many still are. For example, practicing Jews still don't eat pork, and they still celebrate the Sabbath by going to the Temple.

With all of these statutes governing every portion of one's life, it's little surprise that Jews and Gentiles alike are looking at that rulebook and thinking that there's no way anyone would be able to follow all of those—what's the use of trying? Says Rabbi Nechemia Coopersmith, "Imagine stumbling across a gold mine. Would you turn down the gold because you know you won't find ALL the gold mines in the world? That one mine alone will make you rich for life!"

Rabbi Coopersmith emphasizes that despite what many people think, the Jewish faith is a journey. There's not supposed to be a Pharisaic all or nothing mentality that mandates that one get it right the first time.

How To Avoid Religious Brainwashing

Brainwashing can seem especially scary and real when it comes to choosing a religion. So many extremist groups are out their claiming to be the next best thing and the real way to eternal life crop up all the time, and when it comes to matters of faith and spirituality, we are particularly vulnerable. The following are the tips to help you think through a religion or religious group before joining it.

Learn about the religion before signing up. It doesn't make sense to blindly trust that what you've found is definitely the truth just because some people tell you so. They may be right, but for a faith to be your own, you need to consciously choose it yourself. Otherwise you will fall away at the first sign of trouble or discrepancy.

Understand that feelings are subjective and not always trustworthy on their own. Feelings can change based on who is paying attention to you, what you're talking about, whether something is irritating you, or what the weather is like. They are subjective. That said, if your gut is telling you something, don't automatically disregard it, especially if it's telling you to get out now.

Determine what social causes the religion supports and note what the organization's role is in the community. Similarly, investigate possible social or political agendas. Is there any reason to suspect that this religion or church is pushing a political agenda rather than teaching a faith? In most cases, there may be some sort of political thought that is openly talked about or discussed among members, but the political messages don't overwhelm the religious message of the organization.

No matter what stage you are at in your spiritual journey, make a point of going straight to the primary sources for accurate information about what a religion is supposed to be about. Whether it's the Bible, the Torah, the Koran, or the Tantric scriptures, a religious text will be able to clue you in on what the religion is about (if you don't know anything about it or are thinking about converting) and guide you on your journey in a way that is in line with what the religion is about. It's a good thing to compare the teachings in the text with the actions of the religious group. Do they line up? Do they practice what they preach? Is there a good reason why they don't?

Often, the primary religious texts will be long or difficult to understand. Get a good commentary or consult an expert on the matter. Talk about the text with someone from the religious group. This might also be a good way to figure out if the followers of the religion know what they believe or if they are comfortable doing what they are told by the religious leaders. It is also an excellent exercise in learning about your religion for yourself so that if you do encounter a radical extremist group or a cult brainwashing organization, you can identify their lies and avoid being brainwashed.

Learn what enemies or opposition to your faith group is saying about it and figure out their reasoning. While this may seem counterintuitive, like it's opening you up needlessly to a potential manipulative situation or brainwashing tactic, in most cases it does quite the opposite. It will help you understand your beliefs better than you could have without the exploration, and it will make you better equipped to respond when people question you about your faith or try to talk you out of it. Knowing what you believe and why is very important and will continue to be a recurring theme throughout this book. A person who has solid reasons for believing what she believes will be very difficult to brainwash.

Take your time. Spiritual understanding doesn't happen overnight for most people, and when it does, we tend to jump to the conclusion, founded or not, that they might be brainwashed.

Finally, this list isn't exhaustive, but merely a tool to help you along in your religious exploration. Of course there are legitimate overnight conversions that are not the result of brainwashing. Of course there are exceptions to the norms of religious conversion and experience. This book is not large enough for all of those, but it is worth noting that, related to resisting religious brainwashing is what is sometimes thought to be its dark sister, cult brainwashing, which I will talk about in the next chapter.

CHAPTER FIVE: CULTS

Charismatic leader, Jim Jones, started a church in 1954 called the Peoples Temple that stressed egalitarian ideals, providing for the poor, and integrating African Americans into the congregation. To attract more followers and generate revenue to fund his social projects, Jones held healings and conferences that, true to his plan, attracted thousands. In 1960, the organization started a soup kitchen that provided 2800 meals per month (Reiterman, 1982). Other human interest projects included rent support, clothing drives, job placement services, and heating supplies during the winter. Jones and his organization rose to prominence when he was appointed as director of the Indianapolis Human Rights Commission in 1961.

Jones, having studied and practiced the style of Father Divine with the engaging vocal crescendos and diminuendos, captivated his audiences even while preaching things like adopting children and abstaining from sexual activity and spending holidays only with the church family rather than blood relatives. His sermons wove in Marxist thought, drawing similarities between Karl Marx's teachings and the teachings of Jesus Christ, effectively painting Jesus as a communist while refuting a lot of the other Biblical text, unbeknownst to his followers.

Tightening his ranks, Jones demanded that his followers give their possessions to the church community and allow the church to provide for them. Meanwhile, he became convinced that Chicago, and Indianapolis with it, was going to come under a nuclear attack. Thus, he moved the organization and 140 of its members to the Redwoods of California, where it spread to several major cities like San Francisco and Los Angeles. Around this time, he became more open about the fact that the gospel he preached was something called the Divine Principle, which he equated with love, which he in turn equated with socialism.

In 1973, eight members of the Peoples Temple defected, leading to several search parties and a meeting of thirty members at which Jones waved a pistol around declaring that they should all kill themselves because, due to harassment, a socialism group could not exist at that time (Paranoia and Delusion, 1978). Though the suicides were not committed at that time, the organization did begin fake suicide rituals in subsequent years.

In 1974, Jones's organization started renting land in Guyana, which Jones saw as an opportunity to create the perfect socialist community and escape from United States media scrutiny.

By 1976, Jones openly admitted that he was an atheist and had never been interested in faith but in politics. By this point the local police in San Francisco were starting to get suspicious and investigate Jones and his organization, but Jones had gained useful alliances with several local politicians, journalists, and TV reporters who kept him, for the most part, in a positive public light.

In 1977, *New West Magazine* wanted to publish an exposé on the Peoples Temple and its "mixture of Spartan regimentation, fear, and self-imposed humiliation" (Kildruff & Tracy, 1977). The editor of the magazine called Jones the night before the piece was to be published and read the story to him. That night, Jones left for Guyana and over 900 members joined him there, believing that the settlement in Guyana, known as Jonestown, was a paradise free from the sin of the world.

Congressman, Leo Ryan, visited Jonestown on November 17, 1978 to investigate allegations of abuse within the settlement. While he was visiting, several Temple members expressed a wish to leave with Ryan and went with him to the airstrip. Temple security followed them there and opened fire on them, killing the defectors, 3 journalists, and Congressman Ryan.

The following evening, Jones demanded that his congregation drink cyanide in grape Flavor Aid, effectively killing over 900 people, almost a third of whom were children (BBC News, 1978).

A Cult Versus A Religion

Cults are often associated with strange, often dangerous, religious practices. Many assume that all religion is or at some point in history was a cult. According to *Baltimore Sun* writer, Sam Fleischacker, "if your definition of "cult" is a group with a charismatic and very odd leader who thinks he or she has direct access to the divine and spreads a theology that seems both heretical and confused to the established religions around it, then Christianity and Islam and Buddhism were certainly cults when they began—and no doubt the Jews were as well" (2011). Yet, despite their humble origins, none of these major world religions are considered, in themselves, to be cults, though they all have radical offshoots that could be considered cults.

The truth is that the definition of the word "cult" is slippery, and the line between what is religious belief and what is cult brainwashing is a slippery mess, as legislators in several European countries have discovered while trying to establish religious freedom laws (Thompson, 2010). We often think of cults as being related to freaky religious brainwashing practices, but they are not necessarily based in a religion.

Fleischacker concludes that the biggest distinguishing factor between a religion and a cult is about a hundred years. A religion has to stand the test of time. In order to do so, it has to be sustainable for its members. An organization that partakes in destructive or alienating behaviors or requires mass suicides isn't going to be around for a long time for obvious reasons. Cults usually stand out from religions because of the harm they cause to their members.

That said, not all cults are religious in nature.

Tvind a Danish educational cult that initially began as a group of radical young teachers who sought to end racism, inequality, and nuclear power, turned into a traveling group of followers required by their leader, Mogens Amdi Petersen, to put their life savings into a group fund that they weren't allowed access to. Petersen also required them to give all of their free time to the organization and to only work jobs he'd approved of and told them they could work. The organization still continues as somewhat of a mystery to outsiders.

One of Denmark's TV journalists who has made documentaries about Tvind, Thomas Stockholm, says that it's a cult, political organization, and a charity. It's a chameleon (BBC News, 2002). Amdi Petersen disappeared for about 22 years and was found living in a penthouse in Florida while his volunteers lived in dubious conditions around the world. The organization was found to have numerous financial holes and was accused of tax evasion and embezzlement.

Another nonreligious cult is known as Aesthetic Realism. Aesthetic Realism was created by Eli Siegel in 1941 and centered around the idea that happiness comes from liking the world, trying to see the world as it really is, and giving up one's right to see the world from one's own perspective. It claims that people seeing the world from their individual perspective causes feelings of contempt that are the root of all injustice. This doesn't sound too crazy yet, but reading through the organization's "about" page produces a mix of vague sentences worded to sound like philosophy while repeating more or less the same thing multiple times. For example, "Aesthetic Realism, in keeping with its name, sees all reality including the reality that is oneself, as the aesthetic oneness of opposites" (http://aestheticrealism.org/about-us/explanation-of-aesthetic-realism-by-eli-siegel/).

Vague philosophy aside, however, the organization has been referred to as a cult primarily due to the testimonies of its former members, who say that Siegel invited them to show art at his gallery in SoHo and then gave them consultations that sought to manipulate them into agreeing with his ideas. Consultations were taped, and members who refused to succumb to the philosophy of Aesthetic Realism could find the tapes full of their intimate thoughts in someone else's possession (http://michaelbluejay.com/x/).

Members of the group are expected to show a godlike devotion to Siegel's teachings, convert their family members (or abandon their families if they refuse), and admit that if they see anything wrong with Siegel or with Aesthetic Realism, then there is really something wrong with them.

The group is best known in the media for their alleged cure for homosexuality, which consisted of getting homosexuals to swear to

Aesthetic Realism. They stopped talking about the subject of homosexuality when too many cured homosexuals relapsed.

Scientology, often thought to be masquerading as a religion, displays cult-like qualities like mind control techniques, expensive therapy sessions, and dangerous health practices. It lures new followers, who are usually aspiring actors and show people, by promoting the celebrities who are part of it and making claims that it will help people get their lives on track. Through self-help therapy, the church gains access to a person's money and their lives. Famous follower of the Church of Scientology include Tom Cruise, John Travolta, and Kirstie Alley, who receive pampered treatment from the church that its regular members never experience.

The Ku Klux Klan formed in the Civil War aftermath by six men in Pulaski, TN, all of whom were would-be lawyers and former Confederate soldiers. It started out with supposedly harmless pranks in the night wearing white sheets but quickly escalated into a terrorist organization that spanned many states. The purpose of the Klan, according to President Ulysses S. Grant was, "By force and terror, to prevent all political action not in accord with the views of its members, to deprive colored citizens of the right to bear arms and of the right of a free ballot, to suppress the schools in which colored children were taught, and to reduce the colored people to a condition closely allied to that of slavery" (Levitt & Dubner, 2005).

Some other organizations that have been considered to be cults include Amway, The LaRouche Movement, the Center for Feeling Therapy, and Straight, Inc.

What Cults Have In Common

Most cults, whether religious, philosophical, educational, or other, have several similarities that distinguish them from non-cult organizations.

Cults will almost always have a single person who controls the group. The leaders of cults exploit the basic human desire to have respect for authority and peace within a group. Like with the Peoples Temple, there might be an administrative staff who take care of the menial tasks and carry out the leader's mandates, but ultimately, all members are answering to a single person, who in many cases asserts god-like control over their lives.

Cult leaders will often use deception to recruit new followers. Jim Jones used the Christian Church to attract followers and lure them into subscribing to his political ideas about communism. The Yilishen Tianxi Group, which is sometimes referred to as a cult, was an ant farm scam in China that used the Chinese superstition that ants provide mystical healing properties to persuade ignorant Chinese farmers to invest $1375 into an ant farm. The Group would collect the ant corpses after the ants had died, and, theoretically, the profits from the ant products that would then be made would bring the farmers a hefty sum. It didn't quite work out that way, as the ant products didn't do nearly as well as the Group had hoped, and they started using the farmers' investments as part of their own income (Ewing, 2008).

Many cults will try to assert control over even the non-moral parts of your life—who you're allowed to talk to or see, what books you're allowed to read, where you're allowed to work, and what you should be doing with your time or money.

A lot of cults, like the Yilishen Tianxi Group, are primarily interested in your money. They may require that you make an investment in order to join the group or to pool your money and assets into a group fund that only a select few have control over.

Cult followers often use jargon to cover up fallacious or simplistic thinking and, when questioned, won't be able to provide logically sound arguments for what they believe. At the same time, members will often be unable to understand the holes where their philosophy fails to provide adequate answers.

Similarly, cults frequently view everything as either black or white with no gray areas and insist that its members subscribe to this strictly black and white thinking. Gray areas leave room for opinions that don't align with the leader's opinions and thus reduce the amount of control he or she is able to assert over the group.

Resisting the Cults

In the 1960s and 70s, it seemed that outcroppings of religious and political cults were sweeping the nation. Children would disappear for hours, and sometimes days, to return glazed and spouting strange information or to phone their parents denouncing them and claiming that they were joining a Christian commune called the Children of God.

Ted Patrick became a cult brainwashing deprogrammer when he was Governor Ronald

Reagan's Special Representative for Community Relations in southern California in the early 70s. In his book entitled *Let Our Children Go!*, he describes the rampant cult practice of the Children of God cult (1976).

He got a phone call from a distraught parent whose son had been kidnapped by this cult. The police and the FBI had given her the runaround. As a result, he went to find the group. In order to figure out what was going on, he joined up with them, pretending to be a convert, and discovered that thousands of young people were being brainwashed into signing over all of their valuable possessions, including cars, stereos, and bank accounts.

He came up with a plan to kidnap the kids from the cult. Then, he deprogrammed them by responding to their brainwashed statements with correct information, sometimes for days, until they snapped out of their brainwashed state and began using their minds again. He called this deprogramming, a term that would later come to have negative connotations and be renamed exit interviewing.

How to Resist Cult Brainwashing

There are a variety of things that you can do for yourself that will make you more resistant to mind control and brainwashing by cults, many of which center around being confident in your self-worth (McDermott).

Learn not to automatically defer to what others tell you. Ask questions and expect real answers to them. If you are not a child and the person or people in question are not your parents, then, "Because I said so," or, "You wouldn't understand," are not acceptable answers. Someone who is truly an expert in something will be able to explain a concept to anyone, even a child. If you aren't able to get real answers, get out. A real religion, political organization, or human rights group will have a mission statement and a philosophy that hangs together when questioned. A cult will almost always use euphemisms, generalizations, and red herrings to divert a question or will produce philosophy that contradicts itself and therefore does not hang together.

Ask around about the organization if you've never heard of it. Pay attention to any bad press and weigh it against any good press. Pay particular heed to the press surrounding the organization's leader. If he or she is being investigated for fraud or has been accused of sexual crimes, it's wise to flee in the opposite direction.

Be wary if an organization's leaders are demanding or urging or even just suggesting that you give up your life savings or sign over your property to them. A legitimate religion or organization will not ask nonmembers for money right off the bat, or if they do, they will make it clear that it's voluntary. They will not closely question you about your assets or how much money you make at your job. If they do, they don't have your best interests in mind.

You don't have to make decisions immediately. If someone is insisting that you need to decide now or burn in hell, you still retain your right to think about it and make a decision when you're ready. A person telling you otherwise is trying to manipulate you.

Beware of anyone telling you that your problem is your mind or that you think too much and by letting them tell you what you should think you will be free and your life will be better. To quote Admiral Ackbar from Star Wars, "It's a trap!" Of course thinking a lot might create more confusion. In fact, it definitely will at some points in your life, because that's just how thinking works. But thinking for yourself is always better than allowing someone to tell you what you should think and then blindly accepting it.

In fact, passivity is your absolute worst enemy when it comes to people trying to control your mind and beliefs. Strive to actively listen to what people are saying, how they are saying it, and whether there might be ulterior motives present. Be highly suspicious of anyone telling you that you should reject your own feelings or the important people in your life.

Ask for a second opinion from someone you trust. Two or more minds asking the same questions will be stronger than one mind trying to go it alone.

Ultimately, the best thing you can do to resist cult brainwashing and mind control is to know yourself. Learn about your mind and your body and how they relate to each other. Figure out what you believe and why you believe it. Listen to others' thoughts and opinions, but don't automatically adopt them as your own without first putting thought into them and asking yourself if they hang together.

CHAPTER SIX: EDUCATION AND ACADEMIA

In 1997, President Clinton held a White House Conference on Early Childhood Development and Learning, which explored and publicized what happens with the brain growth of children in the first three years of life. This conference proclaimed the importance of funding early childhood development programs stimulating babies and drove a new movement in childrearing that treated every little decision a mother made—from meal preparation to showering—as a high stakes decision.

The Mozart Effect, in which parents thought that listening to Mozart would make their children smarter, was hot, though the studies supporting it were dubious at best. Various products claiming early literacy were appearing on the market. Parents were very keen to do whatever it would take to make their children smarter and more successful later in life.

Into the baby genius phenomenon climate, Julie Aigner-Clark, a stay at home Mom, launched an educational video series called Baby Einstein, a name that made parents believe their children would be smarter if they bought it. Baby Einstein would go on to make her millions of dollars. With an educational spin put on videos for babies, parents no longer needed to feel guilty about putting the baby in front of the TV for an hour or two every day and began to do so more than ever before.

While research at the time could definitively say that stimulation for babies was more important than we had previously thought, there was no research to prove that these videos and electronic toys had any educational benefit whatsoever to babies. In fact, largely due to the ethical implications of testing and running brain scans on children, no evidence existed either proving or disproving the value of educational programming at all, but rather than deterring parents from using what were essentially untested products on their babies, it persuaded them that there couldn't be any harm in trying it out—and didn't they want to give their children the best opportunity there was for genius? "At that point in technology history [the mid 1990s], computers enjoyed a virtually unimpeachable reputation as educational instruments" (Thomas, 2007).

Now, marketers have learned that the best way for toy companies to see financial success is for them to cast their products as educational and advertise their ability to stimulate babies, develop their brains, and in some way promote learning. In her book about the culture of advertising to children, Susan Gregory Thomas interviews a premier children's marketer who says that, "A marketer who establishes 'educational credit' can get away with anything (2007). Leap-Frog, Fisher-Price, and Playskool have jumped on the bandwagon, as have cable networks like Nick Jr. Are the toys, videos, and TV shows actually facilitating learning? It doesn't matter. What matters is that parents, relatives, and friends of babies and toddlers perceive that it will.

In recent years, research on a variety of subjects relating to the mental health and development of babies and toddlers have dug up some disturbing information.

Diane Levin, a professor of early childhood development at Wheelock College says that electronic toys and videos may actually cause a baby to feel sensory overload and check out of the situation in order to cope with it (2001).

Researcher Daniel R. Anderson conducted a study on how television affects babies' focused play and found that having the TV on in the background reduces their concentration on play by half (2005).

Sociologist Juliet B. Schor administered a questionnaire of 150 questions that sought to measure children's involvement with consumer culture and things like self-esteem, depression, anxiety, and health. She found that the more consumer involvement children had (viewing televisions, commercials, etc.), the more likely they were to experience depression, low self-esteem, and psychosomatic symptoms (2004).

According to a report on research findings put out by the American Academy of Pediatrics, there are a variety of negative effects that derive from screen time for children ages 0 to 2. Television before bed causes poor or irregular sleep habits and adversely affects a baby's mood. Heavy media use causes developmental delays in language. Screen time frequently takes away from human interaction and unstructured playtime, which are known to be better for learning and development than media involvement (2011). The AAP recommends that parents minimize screen time for their babies, because the body of research currently available does not show support for the educational value of electronic toys and programming.

Regardless of the increasing number of studies showing the pitfalls of programming for babies and children, marketers have succeeded in appealing to parents' weakest spot—the wellbeing of their children—and manipulating millions every years into purchasing billions of dollars in so-called educational toys and games.

This chapter will address a few of the ways the educational system has brainwashed students, teachers, parents, and community members.

The Feel Good System

In the last few decades, a pervasive ideology of the educational system is that high self-esteem leads to more effective learning. Different state governments have mandated activities that focus on making students feel good about themselves, which take time away from the academic curriculum.

Rather than producing higher levels of academic achievement, this ideology contributed to copious amounts of daily affirmations, but yielded few academic gains. As a result, many colleges have to offer remedial math and reading courses even to high school graduates who graduated in the top third of their classes (Frase & Streshly, 2000).

Grade inflation has become a point of concern, as has the ideology that putting in effort merits a reward. This leaves thousands of high school and college graduates every year who are ill-equipped to deal with the fact that failure is an option outside of school and that feeling good about themselves isn't enough to produce the quality of work that higher education and future employers will expect of them.

This feel-good ideology is more than simply an educational tenet. In *The Truth About Bullshit*, Laura Penny says that the common rhetoric of public discourse is some derivative of, "Everything is okay. You are loved, you are number one, you deserve a break, and the solution to all of your problems is one ideology away." This discourse is present in marketing campaigns, religious institutions, and political campaigns. What it's really saying is, "Don't think too hard about it, and let us help you feel good about who you're becoming."

This discourse encourages people to sit back and take what they view as a well-deserved break from life. When they have so many different institutions and campaigns that are affirming them in their decision to ignore their problems rather than doing something about them, there is virtually no reason for them to work for anything if they are already "number one."

Escapism is increasing with the vast amount of modern day technology. When a person is met with a situation that makes him feel bad about himself, he has no shortage of alternate realities to jump into in order to escape from what he doesn't know how to deal with. Eventually, he will have little need for his actual reality since he feels that his self-esteem is being adequately boosted as it is.

Even certain religious denominations are losing their edge under this feel-good system. Many Christian mega churches, for example, are forsaking their rich theological heritage in favor of a much simpler system that doesn't necessarily hang together, but it makes people feel good about themselves in the moment and come back again next week with their tithes and offerings.

Rather than encouraging attendees to ask questions about their faith and approach study of it from an academic perspective, these institutions are picking and choosing which commandments and stories to preach from the pulpit based on what they believe will please people and contribute to their sense of entitlement and appeal to their goodwill.

Of course we all like to feel good about ourselves, but how can we do so while maintaining personal and academic integrity? One approach is to encourage each other, and especially young people, to meet higher expectations. A paper by the Oregon Department of Education, shows that having high expectations is good for students, because meeting expectations is an excellent contributor to feelings of self-worth (2000).

In fact, students whose teachers have high expectations are less likely to drop out of school and more likely to go on to pursue higher education. High expectations have been shown to build self-esteem, rather than ruin it. Likewise, low-achieving students can rise to the same standards as academically oriented students when they have teachers who are willing to look beyond their label of "low-achieving" and show them that they are equally capable of meeting expectations.

This approach gives students something real to feel good about and teaches them the importance of goal setting to feeling good about themselves and their accomplishments.

Separation of Arts and Sciences, Words and Actions

In Renaissance times, math and art were believed to be inextricably linked, which we can easily see when we look at Renaissance painting and architecture in all of their intricate textures and use of logic, color, and design. Look at the Piero della Francesca's *Legend of the Holy Cross* fresco cycle for awhile and you will start to see, despite the chipping paint, that the entire fresco was expertly constructed using a series of diagonal lines that "cross" each scene in the cycle.

Similarly, take a look at Luca Signiorelli's *Last Judgement* cycle located in the San Brizio Chapel in Orvieto, Italy. Besides the almost science fiction feel of the painting cycle (there are what look like red laser beams shooting from the sky if you turn around and look above the entrance), the most notable thing about it is the way the shadows of each of the figures and buildings in the scenes is painted in direct relation to the real-life window located above the altar. The painting cycle was created for that particular space, and everything from the details of the human bodies to the architecture to the way the light from the window would play on the people if they were really standing there was planned out carefully and with mathematical forethought.

Now, we are taught from a young age to believe that either we must be good at math and science or art or literature. We can get a B.A. degree or a B.S. degree. This detachment is seen in our art and in our math and science. Much of post-modern art lacks mathematical logic, and much of post-modern math (bridges, buildings) lacks art.

Math and science classes are dominating the educational scene as art classes are being pushed out. According to a report published by the U.S. Department of Education, the percent of elementary schools with a visual arts class has declined from 87 percent to 83 percent in the 2009 to 2010 school year (Armario, 2012). The percent of elementary schools with drama classes has decreased even more, from 20 percent to 4 percent. Music classes, however, have only declined in the nation's poorest schools. In the 1999 to 2000 school year, 100 percent of the nation's poorest schools had a music class. A decade later, only 81 percent of those schools still had a music class. It is speculated that the cuts in art departments are due to an increase in the schools' focus on math and reading (Armario, 2012).

Art is no longer considered to be a part of math and science in modern day schools as it once was in Renaissance Italy. Perhaps no one means to say so, but it's like a subtle message is being sent that our generation no longer is interested in building up its own men and women to be as well rounded as Leonardo da Vinci.

On a similar note, a division of rhetorical labor has created an interesting detachment in political discourse. The speechmakers who write the speeches are safe from scrutiny because they don't have to give the speeches, and the speechmakers themselves don't have to think about what they're saying. The speechmakers may receive the judgment and mockery for their speeches, but at least they always have a scapegoat; after all, it is a truth universally acknowledged that no one of any importance writes their own speech these days.

Trouble in Academia

Academics normally need to put their research papers through a peer review process as a sort of quality control for science. This process serves to regulate for researcher bias, unwarranted claims, and validity. If a paper is published in a well-known scientific journal, that means that it's been reviewed by people considered to be experts in the same field. This assures that the information in the paper is reliable and is endorsed by important figureheads. Peer reviews are the checks and balances of academia.

In rare cases, a researcher might choose to skip this step. The 1998 paper by Andrew Wakefield claiming that the MMR vaccine is the cause of autism and bowel disease has since been discredited, as researchers in the field were not able to reproduce the results. In addition, significant financial conflicts of interest were found in Wakefield's experiment along with multiple ethical breaches in the methodology of testing children with autism. Despite the fact that Wakefield's research partners withdrew their support for the paper, it has gone on to cause huge public uproar that resounds today with anti-vaxers proclaiming that "studies show" that vaccines cause autism.

Academic research bias has the power to influence and manipulate results, which, in turn, can influence and manipulate public discourse and opinion. In the case of Wakefield's paper in 1998, his unchecked bias caused numerous parents to refuse a vaccine for their children out of an unprecedented fear of their child(ren) being harmed by it. There is also the matter of statistics in papers and articles that haven't been peer reviewed.

Statistics can be used in many different ways; corporations can alter them to prove a point or to make them look good, researchers can tweak them to fit their bias, and experts can completely make them up, (Marlowe, 1987). Many statistics take the place of common sense and are only there to make people think that the article or paper is more credible than it really is. If a paper has been properly peer reviewed, the statistics have been checked against the existing body of knowledge for accuracy and are, therefore, more trustworthy.

Are Universities Indoctrinating A Leftist Generation?

Ben Shapiro writes in his book entitled *Brainwashed* that 84 percent of Ivy League professors and administrators voted for Al Gore and 9 percent voted for George W. Bush in the 2000 election. He also notes that while 57 percent identified themselves as Democrats, 3 percent said that they were Republicans (2004). Is this a sign that the top American universities are systematically turning out left-leaning students? And if so, is it intentional?

Perhaps there isn't a good way to know this definitively, but it is a widely known fact that liberals certainly seem to dominate the academic scene. One of the aims of higher education is to teach people how to understand other perspectives. This is a good thing in most circumstances. Seeing another's point of view, walking miles or kilometers in another's shoes, is a valuable part of learning and growing both personally and as a society.

The danger is in taking this too far and asserting that there is no such thing as absolute truth and no such thing as good or evil. On the surface, these ideas look pretty, but they fall apart the moment you think about the mass murder of 6 million Jews during the Holocaust or the terroristic bombing of two buildings full of civilians. How could these actions be anything but evil?

We do live in a world that is filled with a lot of subjectivity, but that doesn't mean that there are no absolutes. Think about the laws of gravity and the law of conservation of mass. Think about how the precise tilt of the earth on its axis creates the precise climates that we experience.

If you want an accurate view of the world, then it's important to see the world for both its objectivity and its subjectivity.

Academic Fantasy

According to consumer behavior consultant, Philip Graves, "The lines between science and belief are frequently blurred: elements of dependable science are blended with wishful thinking to create and alluring cocktail of reality and desirable fantasy" (2010). The scientific method and the peer review process prevent many of the fantasy cocktails from parading as reality, though there are some subjects that escape academic scrutiny.

Astrology, for example, combines the science of astronomy with New Age predictions of an individual's future and desires. Astrology has been around for hundreds of years and has been used for everything from predicting an individual's future wealth and success to predicting an entire nation's demise. It's a complicated thing to try to prove wrong, because the results of the prediction are so subjective. It's a little bit like opening a fortune cookie and reading, "You will hope for what you lack." It's so vague that anything could apply. Like with a conspiracy theory, you can easily discard any evidence that doesn't support the prophetic claim and only accept that which does.

Another example of the line between science and fiction being crossed is with alchemy, which is the medieval form of chemistry all about figuring out how to turn metals into gold. For years people believed that this was actually possible. It can most simply be described as a scientific process that would take no small amount of magic to actually work—or a bonafide Rumplestiltskin spinning the straw.

How to Resist Brainwashing and Mind Control in Education and Academia

In the chapters before this one, as well as in the ones after it, you will hear me say that to resist brainwashing, mind control, and negative influence you must educate yourself regarding the information out there. It seems redundant and silly to say in a chapter about resisting academic brainwashing to say that you need to educate yourself about your education in order to resist brainwashing. Yet, there it is. I guess you could say that when it comes to the educational structure and various academic methods and ideologies, you need to meta-educate yourself. What does this look like?

One key way of learning about how education works is to form an understanding and awareness of how different fields of study relate to each other. Nothing ever exists independently of everything else. Art does not exist in a vacuum but within rich cultural heritage and mathematical construction. Music and dance are not independent of science; science speaks to both sound and movement. Politics are always closely related to accounting, and literature and philosophy inform each other. When a school district cuts an art program, they are cutting more than an art program.

Another way to prevent educational brainwashing is to check out the sources yourself when a shocking claim is made. Is the claim made by just one researcher, or are there many saying the same things? Has the study been peer reviewed and published in a reputable journal? Is the method for having obtained the statistics valid, or did it use sample groups that would support a bias in one direction or another?

Similarly, read the actual study and not just the press releases about it. Often the news media get it wrong. For example, a Danish study of women who drank small amounts of alcohol while pregnant found that their children didn't appear to be affected by age 5 (2012). The news media interpreted this to mean that drinking alcohol while pregnant is safe, which the study itself did not claim to prove. In fact, it reiterated the fact that there is no known safe level of alcohol to drink while pregnant.

Finally, make yourself aware of the political leanings of those who are teaching you, as these may subtly influence how they teach you to think. Be just as critical of someone who is telling you that there are no absolute truths as you would be of someone who is telling you that everything is always black and white. Both views can lead you to inaccurately evaluate the situations in which you find yourself and respond to them.

CHAPTER SEVEN: GOVERNMENT AND POLITICS

The Great Firewall of China, also known as the Golden Shield Project, is an attempt by the Chinese Communist Party in China to censor, limit, and monitor the internet use of the people within its borders. Through agreements with search engines like Yahoo! and Google, who are allowed to operate in China only due to having signed a rigid censorship agreement that has not been publicly disclosed, the Chinese government has been able to filter out searches that could be seen as fueling an ideology that opposes the communist government.

Until 2002, websites for the *Washington Post* and the *New York Times* were blocked to all users in the country, and even still, there are filters in place to remove words like "democracy," "Tibet," and "Tiananmen Square massacre" from search results. An estimated 30,000 to 50,000 Chinese internet police exist for the sole purpose of monitoring usage by reading private emails, monitoring chatrooms, deleting blogs with sensitive material, and blocking banned websites. On the most popular sites, a cartoon of a police officer will appear at regular intervals to remind people that they are being watched (Amnesty International, 2008).

The rationale for this censorship is strongly linked with a famous Chinese saying, "If you open the window for fresh air, you have to expect some flies to blow in." While China has become more open about allowing foreign business and investors, the communist government has to be careful about protecting its political ideologies, and therefore must swat some perceived flies by limiting what the people within its borders are allowed to see and say.

Like the Great Wall of China, the Great Firewall is known for its gaping holes and weak points. It's not terribly difficult for the government to block a certain website, but it is fairly difficult for them to keep on top of all of the proxies that people can use to get around the

Firewall to see the website anyway. But while the censorship is faulty at best, it has succeeded in keeping information that could be considered politically inflammatory from people who are not persistent about finding ways around the firewall. Few people are going to accidentally stumble upon information the government isn't okay with them seeing.

Additionally, knowledge of the Firewall's constant surveillance is often enough to cause people to censor themselves without the government stepping in and doing all the work. Saying anything that might be considered anti-government is enough grounds for punishment, and knowing that causes people to be extra careful about what they say in their personal emails and social media. To keep people on edge and censoring themselves, the laws governing what is and isn't allowed to be viewed online are purposefully vague.

Cyber cafés, where people often go to use the internet when they can't afford it at home are monitored very closely. People need to give their full names and ID in order to be allowed to use a computer. Because they fear being shut down, these cyber cafés will frequently have additional censorship software installed as a means of keeping people from bending the rules.

The Cold War and Fear of Brainwashing

The 1950s Cold War saw the biggest communist scare in United States history. Fear of being brainwashed by communists was all over the news media, and, as a result, all over the United States of America. People feared being converted to communist ideas without even realizing it.

At that time, "American troops were being killed and captured by the thousands in Korea. Panic spread that China's Communists had learned how to penetrate and control the minds of American prisoners of war" (Weiner, 2008). American prisoners of war were being found having been brainwashed by their captors. The knowledge that this kind of thing could actually happen and the widespread press about the happenings helped to facilitate a communist scare in the United States of epic proportions. Many war vets returning from the war were suspected of brainwashing and were closely watched by the government.

The United States government conducted surveillance of suspected communist informants to the Soviet Union in the United States. The media helped spread the fear that it was plausible and very likely that the communists could and would take over the country. Anyone who openly sympathized with communist ideas was hounded by the law, alienated from friends and family members, fired from their job, and accused of being a communist revolutionary.

The 1950s communist scare is a great example of how rampant, unfounded fear can influence a nation of people to abuse civil freedoms like the basic freedom to join a political party and express beliefs that differ from the state government. But then again, think back to chapter five when we talked about the Peoples Temple and Jim Jones, and that's enough to see that the scare wasn't completely unfounded, though in the 50s, Jones hadn't yet made his mark.

Government Conspiracy Theories

There are a million conspiracy theorists with blogs on the internet that declare that the government is brainwashing us, controlling us, and otherwise out to get us. By their very nature, conspiracy theories are impossible to prove or disprove, often using circular reasoning, purely anecdotal evidence, and hypothetical arguments. This book is not big enough to thoroughly investigate the validity of every claim that the government is spying on our personal lives in order to brainwash us, that it causes huge natural disasters like Hurricane Katrina, or that a certain president is actually the antichrist.

That said, it is worth taking a look at signs that point to a conspiracy theory being false (Shermer, 2010). A conspiracy theory is likely to connect causally unrelated events in a series of dots that can only be explained by the theory itself. It will likely seem to arbitrarily assign meaning to events that have no real significance. The people behind the conspiracy are unlikely to be able to pull off the conspiracy due to the fact that they are not a superhero. The conspiracy is ultimately supposed to end in nation or world domination that is the result of large numbers of people needing to keep a lot of secrets.

You might be talking with a conspiracy theorist if the person has an inability to distinguish between facts and speculations and refuses to consider, let alone accept, possible alternative options to the conspiracy theory. He will accept only evidence that supports the theory and reject evidence that doesn't.

Conspiracy theories are interesting to think about. The small number of them that have been found to be true have been sufficient evidence for a conspiracy theorist to point to them and say, "Well, Watergate happened, therefore what I'm saying is valid." Be observant when talking with overly suspicious people about politics, and don't allow yourself to accept outrageous ideas without questioning them first.

Capitalist Politics

Is capitalism with its free market the best economic system? And are we brainwashed if we think it is? It's true that, as Americans, we have a few hundred years of history to back up the gospel of capitalism and influence our opinions, and that it might be objectively better than many other forms of government that deliberately and systematically oppress their people and keep the poor poor and the rich even richer. It's not *1984*, despite what conspiracy theorists might claim.

If we take a close look at capitalism, however, we see that it is, at its most absolute, a ruthless power that leads to monopolies and oligopolies that have the power to say how much a resource is going to cost and limit its availability based on whether people are demanding it. This system serves to benefit a few, while keeping the masses at the mercy of the whims of the few.

The word "competitive" is important here, because competition is what keeps companies continually trying to improve themselves as well as keeping prices within reasonable boundaries. The competitive part of American capitalism is what American people love, because it is what keeps the doors of opportunity open to entrepreneurs with new ideas, or changes to old ideas, who have the gumption to test them out. Think Henry Ford. Think Sam Walton. Think Amazon. The opportunity to be great has been an important part of the development of the United States as a nation. We have always loved a good story about the underdog rising to success and overcoming unspeakable odds to do so. While pure capitalism keeps people within their classes largely unable to move from one level to the next, the mixed economy capitalism that the United States economy practices is usually a better way to keep people, not necessarily on equal footing, but with the potentiality for equal footing.

Unfortunately, even free market competitive capitalism can't be a perfect system, because human nature doesn't allow it, just like human nature doesn't allow for a philosophically pure form of communism, though many countries and organizations have certainly tried with varying levels of success—China, the Soviet Union, and even the Amish people to some extent have practiced the communalistic living of the communist structure and had it come up flawed. The fact is that people aren't always satisfied with adequately meeting their needs. There are always people who want more than what everyone else has got, whether that's power or money or reputation. No system can eliminate human nature from the mix. Overall, it can be argued that American capitalism, such that it is, is the system that best accounts for the inevitability of human greed.

As a capitalist economy filled with people who operate via the pig principle, which states that people have an insatiable desire to always have more, it's pretty safe to say that no matter what the political party is, government officials and politicians are operating based on what's going to bring them the biggest net gain. Money is a huge motivator, and getting the people in office who will get one the most money plays a huge part in every election.

On an individual level, that's the same thing we do come election time, though most of us are doing it on a much smaller scale. We want to vote for the candidate or party that most closely aligns with what we perceive to be our best interests.

Not only that, but regardless of what political party you look at, everyone is thinking in terms of getting the people into office who will push a certain agenda, whether it's legalizing marijuana, abortions, or bestiality. Political parties go to great expense to market themselves in attractive ways so that the general public will vote for them and their agendas with them. In many ways, they are not much different than a brand of beer or a type of laundry detergent. Perhaps the most notable difference is that they approve this message.

As advertising for products took an upswing in the 1950s, politicians began to take notice and enlist the services of advertisers in order to market their candidates and ideas in the most appealing ways possible. If corporations could manipulate good public opinion and emotions in order to sell a soft drink or a soap brand, then certainly the politicians could do the same thing. Since then, election campaigning has been a game of how much money one party or another is willing to spend on manipulating the public.

When television was becoming a fixture in American homes around the time of the 1960 presidential election, the screen made a huge difference in the way political campaigns were run. Now the rhetoric was not the only thing that mattered. Looks were a factor now as well. John F. Kennedy beat out incumbent Richard Nixon for president in the 1960 election not in small part due to his fantastic TV presence during the presidential debates. His looks and charisma persuaded many to vote for him over the less physically appealing Richard Nixon, even if his arguments weren't quite as thoughtful. Many believed that if it hadn't been for the new medium, John F. Kennedy wouldn't have won.

How Do We Know Who's Right?

It may seem like an impossible task to figure out who to vote for in any state or national election, but here are a few ideas to help you make sense of all the propaganda. First, be sure to read and watch a story from multiple different sources of varying political leanings. You'll never get the whole picture just by watching Fox News or the Daily Show. Political parties have put a lot of thought into framing their campaigns in ways that make them look good and the other side look bad. Getting the story from all perspectives will clue you in on the politically charged vocabulary. For example, conservatives who are against legalizing abortion will say that they are pro-life (insinuating that liberals are anti-life), while the liberals will say that they are pro-choice (insinuating that the conservatives are against making their own free choices).

Become aware of the many false dichotomies presented in politics. "If you don't support gay marriage, then you must hate gay people," is what the liberal agenda wants you to believe, but take a step back and ask yourself if hating homosexuals is really the only reason why someone might not support gay marriage, and, moreover, if it's even fair to assume that those who don't support gay marriage must necessarily hate gay people.

Make a point of asking people you know what they think about different issues and why. There's nothing wrong with a little debate or disagreement as long as it's respectfully managed. Getting a good understanding of what others believe might sway you to their side if they make a compelling argument for their perspective. Usually, however, learning about the other side's perspective simply gives you a better understanding of where they're coming from, what's valid and what's not, and where your own argument gets weak. Knowing the other side's case will protect you from the fallacy of building up straw men and tearing them down in a ridiculous manner that makes you look like you didn't quite finish your research.

Figure out what you personally want to get out of an election and figure out which candidate's goals are most in line with what you want and believe. Read personal statements of each candidate. If you know what you want out of an election and have a pretty good idea of which party will come closest to providing that (there are rarely perfect matches), then you won't be as likely to succumb to the "He has better hair" argument that people make in the booth on voting day when they haven't done their research.

CHAPTER EIGHT: MILITARY

Propaganda is as much a part of wars as guns are. It's the emotional weapon of the military. It can succeed where guns are powerless. It can inspire where speeches might fail. For example, in World War 2, pornographic propaganda dropped by Germans on American soldiers. It was meant to make them miss their wives and girlfriends at home and lose morale. Interestingly, it actually increased moral, because the male soldiers were excited by the dirty pictures rather than worried that their significant others were turning to the arms of other men. Wartime propaganda isn't just for political effect but also for emotional effect.

In more recent years, propaganda has had a large role in the War in Afghanistan both from the United States military and the Afghan insurgents. The United States Military Information Support Operations (MISO) units in Afghanistan, sometimes known as Psychological

Operations (PSYOP), with the mission of "Influencing the hearts and minds of the people." Perhaps in many ways, it doesn't yet live up to its mission, but its aim was to reach out to the local civilians and inspire them to feel a sense of national pride, and to support their government. It did this in a variety of ways, from organizing clothing donations for the children to sitting down with the local families to eat and talk to creating and distributing propaganda to civilians to aid the war effort, spread word about the dangerous things the Taliban was responsible for, inspire patriotism for their own country's leadership, and build good will towards the leadership within the local communities.

In order to distribute a message that would be effective in gaining support for a particular mission, analysts were sent into communities to research the way the local people think and perceive and what their vulnerabilities are. Once the analysis is done, a product goes through a series of steps including development and testing. Care must be taken in the development and content of these projects, because there's always a chance that the propaganda could be seen by the entire world and assumed to be the United States policy.

MISO propaganda can fall under several different categories: While PSYOP is an official statement made and overtly distributed by the United States government often through loudspeakers and face to face communication; Gray PSYOP is an intentionally gray area in which the source of the information distributed is designed to look ambiguous or possibly coming from a local, nonviolent source; Black PSYOP creates materials that appear to come from a hostile source, the Taliban for example, is considered to be a function separate from the United States government, and is kept top secret due to the sensitive information that is often divulged.

The use of comics in the War in Afghanistan was found to be especially successful, as the local people really liked them. Missions into the villages with interpreters took place in order to win the peoples' emotional support. These were often a vital part of persuading people to support their country and reject the former oppressive government.

However, the Afghan insurgents were able to produce more effective propaganda than the United States PSYOP, because they did not have to put it through the rigorous and time-consuming chain of command and approval that the United States military had in place. They could, therefore, distribute materials more quickly with less concern about telling the truth. They also had a home team advantage, which included greater access to local news media outlets that would be able to most easily sway public opinion.

It was an information war more than any other war in history. The fight was in the print and in the media. It was psychological, and the goal was to leave the Afghani people and their country stronger and better off than they had been before.

Of course, it wasn't an easy battle. On numerous occasions, insurgents destroyed civilian property and lives and then sent out propaganda through news media and pamphlets blaming the violence on United States soldiers in order to inspire civilian hatred and distrust of the United States military. On a similar note, when the U.S. Army had an accident of any kind, the insurgents were able to exaggerate it to the public in order to further sway their opinions and loyalties.

Impressionable Afghan children were told that the U.S. military was bad and encouraged to attack the U.S. bases by throwing rocks, stealing things, and concealing weapons.

The War in Afghanistan didn't have the decisive victory of the World Wars. Many are unsure whether to count it a success or a failure. Some people were empowered, and the government was shifted from one corrupt group to another.

Is It Worth It?

"We created school supplies, collected winter clothes for the kids, and brought them snacks. They'd run up to us with their arms outstretched when they saw us, expecting that we would give them something," says one war vet. They did good things for the communities they were stationed in.

Yet, the intense military atmosphere on deployment could play with soldiers' emotions and make them lose faith in their mission and in humanity. For a soldier in Afghanistan, engaging with the Afghan people over and over and seeing the same bad stuff in such a short period of time, it wasn't hard to convince oneself that that's all there was. They would give a little girl a lollipop and then watch a boy beat the girl up because he wanted it.

Soldiers could, essentially, brainwash themselves into a cynicism that comes from watching people being destructive and violent to each other. They could easily forget what makes a human a human and that underneath all of the violence were people who needed help.

Most of the time, the difference between an effective and an ineffective soldier is the ability to remember what makes a human a human and to look people in the eye instead of falling under cynicism's harsh glare.

Training to Conform: Is Altruism a Form of Brainwashing?

Many people from the military have drawn correlations between the military and a cult. While some say that the military teaches discipline, responsibility, and respect for people outside of oneself, others say that it's textbook brainwashing that teaches conformity and strips one of all individuality and personal identity. Soldiers stand the same way, walk the same way, dress the same way, and respond to authority the same way.

Additionally, the military—not just the American military—uses scare tactics and group punishments to encourage conformity to the group for the greater good. A person is more likely to fall in line with instructions if not doing so results in everyone else's punishment as well.

Required curriculum teaches about the great history of the group, and drills include exercises meant solely to learn how to listen better to instructions from the leaders. While many frown on the military conformity training and treat it like an injustice, there is certainly something to be said for learning how to function as a member of a larger group.

It is also true that, especially in America, many of us have an overdeveloped sense of individuality and worth in relation to others. While many (particularly eastern) cultures value face-giving techniques (saving face for others), the western world primarily focuses on saving face for the individual. The persisting face-saving thought makes it more difficult to accept that it's not always brainwashing to act for the good of a group, even if it means risking one's own self.

Risking one's life for the good of others is otherwise known as altruism. As soldiers train for war, they inevitably think, in some way, about altruism.

Ways To Resist Military Brainwashing

It's questionable how many useful resources are available to would-be soldiers before signing up, particularly if you are a woman. Many soldiers, especially female ones, say that they had no idea what to expect during training. They had no idea what to expect when it came to living primarily with a large group of men. They didn't know how they would be treated by the men in their units or how prevalent sexual harassment would be for them.

Whether you are a man or a woman signing up for the military, do your best to figure out what you're getting into. Talk to people who have recently experienced training. The magical world of the internet is at your fingertips to research books and articles about relevant military experiences as well as to get in contact people who might be able to mentor you.

Expect that training is going to be hard, both physically and emotionally. Showing up to basic training, it's unfair to expect that those in charge of you are going to care about your personal opinions on a subject that they themselves have worked hard to excel at. It's also unrealistic to expect that anyone will ask you how you are

One of the best gifts you can give to yourself before beginning your military career is to be secure in yourself. If you know who you are and what you believe, it will help you resist becoming just another brainwashed soldier in a vast sea of them. The real you is who you are on the inside when you're by yourself. That's not something that a strict dress code and muscle depleting amounts of exercise can strip you of. Strive to know yourself while deriving all of the benefits that the training offers you.

When you are overseas, resist the brainwashing that you can do to yourself as a result of desensitization by remembering the humanity in everyone. When asked what she did to keep this from happening to her, one war vet told me, "I ate food with the locals. I drank chai with them. I'd go to their homes and bring an interpreter with me so that I could talk with them about their families and their interests. I looked them in the eye and sat with them. You need to talk to them without your hand on your weapon or your helmet or gloves on." Thinking of the local people as the enemy only fuels disillusionment.

CHAPTER NINE: MEDICAL INDUSTRY

Lobotomies in the middle of the twentieth century were a form of literal brainwashing popular in mental institutions to alter the behavior of the most difficult patients. A lobotomy is a psychosurgical procedure that destroys neural connections in the frontal and prefrontal cortex.

Neurosurgery as a treatment for mental illness and behavior disorders began in the 1890s when a German physiologist named Friedrich Goltz removed sections from the neocortexes of dogs. He said in (Finger, 2001), "I have mentioned that dogs with a large lesion in the anterior part of the brain generally show a change in character in the sense that they become excited and quite apt to become irate. Dogs with large lesions of the occipital lobe on the other hand become sweet and harmless, even when they were quite nasty before."

Goltz's studies on dogs led physician and asylum director Gottlieb Burkhardt to try a similar operation on 6 of his schizophrenic patients. One of these patients died within a week of the operation, and another committed suicide. Though the other surgeries appeared to have been successful, the resulting public outcry caused him to cease operating on more patients.

In the 1930s Antonio Egas Moniz took another stab at human lobotomies after learning about lobotomies done on chimpanzees by Yale researchers Carlyle Jacobsen and John Fulton. Moniz first operated on a manic depressive patient by drilling holes on either side of her skull, injecting absolute alcohol into the white matter, and moving an inserted knife back and forth inside, effectively severing the nerves connecting the frontal cortex and the thalamus (Mo, 2007). He reported that the patient seemed calmer and less paranoid and anxious than she had before. He went on to operate on about 50 other people with varying results.

American neuroscientist, Walter Freeman, attended one of Moniz's symposiums on the frontal lobe and then brought the lobotomy to the United States shortly thereafter. He refined Moniz's technique, but, after declaring the procedure to be too messy and time consuming, he created a new technique, called the ice pick technique or the transorbital lobotomy, that required neither anesthesia nor a hospital stay afterward. In this technique, an instrument resembling an ice pick was inserted above the eyes and swished around in the brain tissue. With this new technique, the lobotomy became an in and out procedure in January of 1945.

But like the prior surgeries, Freeman's also had varying results. Sometimes his patients could go back to work immediately following, and sometimes they were rendered severely incapacitated. Nonetheless, Freeman, who liked the show, traveled around the United States performing lobotomies in front of audiences and teaching unqualified psychiatrists how to perform them. The journalists who followed him around on these tours gave him a lot of press, thus popularizing the lobotomy as an inexpensive means of treating all kinds of mental illness.

It was performed on 40,000 patients in the United States largely because there was no other known treatment, and also because the mental institutions were filling up and becoming a more and more expensive way to treat mental illness. Lobotomies were used on the criminally insane, prisoners, and as a cure for political dissidents and behavioral issues.

Perhaps one of the more shocking lobotomy cases was that of Howard Dully, whose stepmother had him lobotomized when he was twelve in December of 1960 because of his supposed defiant behavior. While other doctors told Lou Dully that there was nothing wrong with her stepson, Freeman was eager to perform the surgery. When the procedure didn't render young Dully a vegetable, his stepmother had him turned over as a ward of the state, where he had a very difficult time getting his life in order and dealing with the pain of feeling like a freak without understanding why as well as the knowledge that his father would have allowed this to happen to him.

The popularity of lobotomies waned in the late 1960s, as negative results were becoming known and recognized and drug treatments were on the rise.

Wives Tales and Things Even Doctors Believe

In a study done by Dr. Rachel Vreeman and Dr. Aaron Carroll (2007) and published in the *British Medical Journal*, a few of the most common medical myths were explored for validity and found to be false. For example, medical professionals have long believed that hair and fingernails grow for a little while after death. In reality, they do not. It is the body's rapid dehydration process shrinking skin by the roots of the hair and around the fingernails that makes it appear as though they do.

Another myth, likely inspired by people wanting to break into the self-improvement field, is that people only use 10 percent of their brains. MRI and PET scans have revealed that this is false. Except in the event of a serious brain injury, there are no dormant sections of the brain.

A very popular belief that finds its way around social media every time a new hit diet book comes out is that a person should, on average, drink 8 glasses, or 64 ounces, of water per day. Vreeman and Carroll did some looking into this myth and discovered that there is no scientific evidence that supports this, though there is a recommendation from the 1945 Nutritional Council recommended 8 glasses of *fluid* in a day. This would include the juices from fruits and vegetables, coffee, tea, and whatever liquid you might cook into your dinner.

They also explored whether tryptophan in turkey actually causes more sleepiness than another other meat. They discovered that turkey has the same amount of tryptophan every other bird meat has and concluded that a few reasons why we might perceive greater sleepiness on Thanksgiving Day when we eat turkey could be that we eat a greater amount of food than we usually do, and we often drink alcohol. Overeating and drinking alcohol are both known to be causes for sleepiness, and in this case are more likely to be causing the extra sleepiness on Thanksgiving than the turkey is.

While these medical myths are, for the most part, harmless, it's good to be aware that sometimes what we've always assumed to be common knowledge is not the truth. This was never clearer than when looking at the Rockefeller drug monopoly that started in the early twentieth century.

The Rockefellers and the War on Drugs

The Rockefeller Foundation joined ranks with the AMA and the Carnegie Foundation at the start of the twentieth century in the name of philanthropy and put its money into universities and drug-based research that would eventually be the basis of controlling the entire drug industry. The money donated to schools came with strings attached and gave the Rockefellers leverage in the academic fields. This leverage was used to influence the course of study and eliminate all studies that were not in line with the goal of lining the Rockefeller family bank accounts.

This medical research earned them huge monetary returns from the medical drug industry. Because the Rockefellers stood to lose money if they allowed development of alternative cures to cancer and other serious medical issues, they suppressed organizations like Royal Rife cancer cure in order to secure their coffers. They also started feeding a myth that natural treatments and plant medicines are akin to witchcraft and don't work the way drugs do.

Seeing a cornerstone with the narcotics industry, the Rockefellers worked hard to gain complete control of it. They enlisted the help of trouble-making religious groups, the media that were under their control due to strategic funding, and their impressive political clout to help get marijuana, hemp, and narcotics prohibited from the general public, thus making them the only way to obtain the drugs.

In addition, several anti-marijuana films came out around this time, fueling public opinion that marijuana is dangerous and destructive. "[S]everal films like 'Reefer Madness' (1936), 'Marijuana: Assassin of Youth' (1935), and 'Marijuana: The Devil's Weed' (1936)…were all propaganda films designed by these industrialists to create an enemy out of marijuana. Reefer Madness was possibly the most interesting of the films as it depicted a man going crazy from smoking marijuana and then murdering his family with an ax. With all of these films, the goal was to gain public support so that anti-marijuana laws could be passed without objection" (Martino, 2012). Thus, despite many years of safe over the counter cannabis use by ordinary people for basic aches and pains—headaches, menstrual cramps, muscle spasms—the masses were being effectively brainwashed into demonizing the medicine.

When the prohibition laws were put in place in the late 1930s, the Rockefellers effectively had control over physicians and their practices. Narcotics, after all, are painkillers, and doctors need them to treat patients. Instead of being able to get narcotics on their own to treat their own aches and pains, people had to go see doctors to write them a prescription for the expensive drugs of which the Rockefellers were the gatekeepers.

The illegalization of marijuana in the United States has had a lasting effect on public opinion in relation to the drug as well as on the sorts of punishments that are given for being found by law enforcement with it in hand. In order to enforce the marijuana prohibition, law enforcement had to crack down hard on those who used it, the effects of which we still see today. "The consequences are often surprisingly drastic and completely disproportionate to the offense. Every aspect of a person's life can be impacted by a marijuana arrest, including eligibility for public housing and student financial aid, job opportunities, child custody and even immigration status" (NYCLU, 2015). This is awfully extreme for possessing a drug that is less harmful than alcohol and most other illegal drugs.

Additionally, the Rockefellers have been a force behind driving disease scares and then following the scares up with savior drugs. This makes them look like society's heroes while they're cashing in on the fear.

While the Rockefellers' influence still resounds in the medical and educational field today, there are some key improvements that have been made. For example, chiropractors and massage therapists who are trained to realign the body and work out its tensions are finding increasing success and popularity, as these solutions often fix recurring pain without the use of drugs, which only mask pain.

Additionally, while for years it has been assumed that doctors should study only the medical drug related cures, seeking out learning from Doctor of Optometry schools that teach holistic and natural medicine is on the rise. Whether this is because they are, at present anyway, easier to get into than the traditional medical field or because young people are starting to become more conscious of and interested in natural ways to heal the body is unclear, but this is certainly a change in the right direction that hasn't come too soon.

Futuristic Brain Manipulation

Brain circuit manipulation and brain drugs have found some recent news coverage, though they have a long way to go before they will be effective in manipulating public opinion.

The US National Institutes of Health (NIH) issued a report entitled, "Interim Report: Brain Research through Advancing Innovative Neurotechnologies (BRAIN) working group" in September of 2013. "The report has extensively examined President Barack Obama's brain project, which mentions the need to develop electromagnetic modulation as a new technology for brain circuit manipulation," said the Asian Human Rights Commission (2013).

These new technological developments might be a new weapon of mass destruction or mass control, some are saying. Others are saying that they will be used by the government to alter criminal thoughts and control emotions, the subconscious, and dreams. A microchip called RNM, or Remote Neural Monitoring "is a controversial technology which is being used in many countries for security maintenance and surveillance" (Hassam). It can monitor and control sleep patterns and send messages to various parts of the brain while bypassing other senses. Besides the obvious question of whether RNM violates human rights, another concern includes potential cancerous effects resulting from the proximity of the device's microwaves to the brain tissue.

While some new brain technologies are still in prototypical stages and have yet to find success in human brains, this is certainly a field to sit up and pay attention to for the deep moral and ethical implications it will have, and already has had, down the road lest we all find ourselves as pawns in the real life Matrix.

Unbrainwashing and the Medical Field

Because the medical field is so specialized and full of jargon and complicated science that, let's face it, not all of us have the base knowledge to read and understand, it can be complicated to figure out facts from fiction when it comes to medical brainwashing and attempts at manipulation.

Here's some advice that applies particularly when trying to sort out medical issues.

First of all, know that if you receive a diagnosis from one doctor that you feel unsure about, you are always free to seek out a second opinion from another doctor or medical institution before you start a treatment. If multiple experts are separately telling you the same thing, there's a strong chance that they're right.

When you hear something that you think sounds crazy or that is surrounding in controversy, like the anti-vaccination movement claiming that childhood vaccines cause autism, go straight to the studies. First, ask if the study you are looking at has been peer reviewed. If not, take what you read with a grain of salt. Pretty much all scientific research will have three sections that are fairly readable for non-experts as long as you have some time to sit down and dig in. These are the abstract, which will give you a summary of what the paper is about; the introduction, which will give you the history of studies done previous to the one you are reading that the researchers of this project will have read and studied before beginning their own study; and the conclusion or discussion section, which will explicate for you in greater detail than the abstract what the study found and any biases or errors that occurred during the course of the study. The wordings can be overly academic and stuffed, but the more material you read like this, the faster and better you will be able to catch on in the future.

The other sections (the methodology and the results) detail what the experiment entailed and all the numbers and charts associated. If you are very gung ho about reading these, go for it, but summaries of these will be present in the three more readable sections of the paper.

Be cautious about studies you hear about on the news or read as a sensational new Yahoo! News story, as the news station or paper or website may have a certain bias that they might be trying to put across to viewers and readers, despite the fact that it might be inaccurately slanting the study and forcing conclusions where they were never made. Headlines are designed to intrigue you. The stories that follow them don't always warrant them. If you're curious about the validity of a sensational statement made on the news, check out the research before you spread the word.

With the Ebola and Anthrax scares and the flu vaccine shortage scares being reported on daily, it might be tempting to allow yourself to be swept along with the public panic. Evidence shows that as of November of 2014, of the eight cases of Ebola treated in the United States, only one has died (Urbanski). Of course, one death from Ebola is one death too many to be sure, but compared with the amount of fear the media managed to inspire in our hearts, the chances that anyone else would get the virus were slim to none. The Anthrax and flu vaccine shortage were similar. Remember that the media want an interesting story, and they will repeat the same story from slightly different angles for as long as it makes them money. Basically, calm down. If the area of the scare is near where you live, take precautions, and then take everything else with a grain of salt.

CHAPTER TEN: CORPORATIONS

As of June of 2015, Amazon has decided to pay authors royalties for ebooks self published through Kindle Direct Self Publishing Select program based on how many pages a reader actually reads rather than on the number of books purchased by readers. Under the old system, a pool of money was kept for these authors and divvied up based on the number of downloads and borrows each book got. Amazon argues that it wants to do a better job of dividing up the money based more on how long their work is and whether buyers actually read each page. This has created an uproar both among Amazon's self-published authors and its readers for a variety of reasons.

First of all, many authors feel jipped, because now even if a customer pays for their book, they won't see any profit on it unless the customer actually opens the book and starts flipping pages. Those in the writing industry also fear that this new policy will change the way the books are written. Will writers deliberately write longer books in order to increase profit potential? *Atlantic* writer, Peter Wayner, thinks that writing probably will change, but it won't necessarily be for the worst. Rather than having to pad a book with fluff to make it carry more weight on a bookstore shelf, he says that, "A system with per page payouts is a system that rewards cliffhangers and mysteries. It rewards anything that keeps people hooked" (2015).

Second of all, fans of these self-published authors lose some of their power to support the authors they want to support. Friends and family members of an author might not personally be enamored with the genre an author is writing in, but they care about that author and want to show their support for his career nonetheless. Traditionally, these people could go to the store or the online venue, purchase the book, and thus contribute a small amount of money to support that author. They might never read the book, but that's their choice. Now, with the pay per page ruling, if the book isn't read, the purchase doesn't support the author.

Furthermore, the readers don't have the option of only paying for what they read—they still pay full price whether they read the whole book or not—and Amazon taking an equal hit for the number of pages not read.

Thirdly, there's the whole issue of personal privacy. Unlike traditional publishing companies, Amazon has full access to the number of pages individual customers read. While Random House can't walk into your home and check where your bookmarks are in each of their books on your shelf, Amazon can march into your Kindle do that very thing. The amount of data mined from Amazon customers is truly astounding and walks a potentially dangerous line of personal privacy and a self-serving corporate agenda.

What kind of influence can Amazon have on peoples' purchasing and reading habits with all of this personal information? When you purchase a book, Amazon can tell you what other people who purchased the same book are also buying, putting the idea into you head that you might want that item too.

In 2010, Amazon joined forces with Facebook, which allowed Amazon not only to monitor what you are buying and listening to, but to compare it with what all of your friends are buying and listening to. That's why ads from Amazon pop up on your Facebook page telling you how many of your friends liked or bought a certain item. "It's data mining meets peer pressure at its finest" (Lindstrom, 2011). Amazon has the power to subtly persuade you to buy what it appears everyone else is buying.

We Three Kings of Capitalism

The United States is a capitalist economy, and that makes corporations the kings. Corporations have the ability to steal our money while making us believe that it was all our idea. The economic boom in America after the Second

World War fed a desire to create new products, which in turn caused corporations to turn what used to be war propaganda ideas into consumerist propaganda aimed at making the increasing middle class buy more stuff than ever before.

Extensive market research combined with an increasing body of psychological and human behavioral studies has helped marketers refine the persuasion process to give corporations what they have now: the sly ability to use emotions and human nature to influence purchasing decisions. It's brilliant but scary the way a company can predict how most people will respond to something as simple as a color change, a moral insinuation, a facial expression, a greeting, or the placement of a shelf in a store.

Philip Graves cites a study by Paco Underhill, which found that the number of customers who decided to buy something increased by half when a staff member at the store greeted the customer (2010).

Think about the billion-dollar baby products industry. Companies prey on nervous expectant parents' fear that they will be bad parents by telling them that they need to purchase the best, which means the most expensive, products for their unborn children. Of course the baby doesn't care if the stroller brand is Bugaboo or Babyroues or even so used you can't even see the brand label anymore for heaven's sake, but somehow advertisers can make parents feel obligated to buy the more expensive brand lest their child suffer under the hardship of not having the same caliber of stroller that all of the other babies have.

Not only do corporate entities manipulate the minds and emotions of consumers, but they also manipulate and control those of their own employees. That is, employees who want to keep their jobs will learn to do what they're told and keep opinions that diverge from the corporate mainstream to themselves.

Fake Reviews and the Benefit of Polarized Opinions

With the advent of online purchasing, authors and their supporters are able to create fake book reviews to create a buzz about their book. The idea is that customers who see the multiplicity of positive reviews on an item will then be more likely to buy the book. It's peer pressure on a national and international level. A hundred people liked this book, therefore it must be good.

Successful crime writer, Stephen Leather, admitted to using sock puppet accounts in an interview panel discussion with Steve Mosby. He said, "I'll go onto several forums, from the well-known forums, and post there, under my own name and under various other names and various other characters. You build this whole network of characters who talk about your books and sometimes have conversations with yourself. And then I've got enough fans…" (Charman-Anderson, 2012). He's not the only author who does this, but he argues that unlike authors who have an entire publishing company's marketing team creating a buzz for them, a self published author has got to do what he's got to do in order to get book sales and have any shot at all of continuing to write and feed himself.

Creating a buzz means causing consumers to think in this manner, which, in turn, affects sales. Sometimes the buzz created is overwhelmingly positive. Other times, an author will understand that it's not just the extremely positive reviews that will drive business, but any reviews that are polarized and create hype.

Creating a buzz isn't necessarily about making everyone like something, but about acknowledging the fact that people are different, and as such they will not all like the same things. Christian Rudder, in his book *Dataclysm*, which is about big data in social media, particularly in his online dating site OkCupid, talks about the power of posting a photo that polarizes opinions. When a lot of people love a photo and a lot of people hate it, more buzz is created. The man or woman who markets him or herself this way, will receive more messages than the one who posts a nice photo that doesn't stand out from the crowd (2014).

You may have heard the adage that all press is good press. While that's not strictly true—getting a lot of mediocre reviews isn't likely to drive your sales—bad press is generally thought of in as positive of a light as overly enthusiastic reviews, from a marketing standpoint. Controversy sells. People like to take sides and have an opinion.

This is a good thing to keep in mind when reviewing a business online. Giving a two or three star rating may have more negative consequences on a product as subjective as a book than writing a nasty one star review. After all, creating buzz doesn't have to mean creating an excess of positive hype.

Monopoly and the Game of Life

In the late nineteenth century, the famous diamond corporation, De Beers, began taking control of the diamond trade, effectively monopolizing the industry and making the decisions about how expensive diamonds were and what qualities to sell, and how many diamonds to make available for purchase. People who wanted to buy diamonds were at the mercy of the De Beers corporation as far as price and quality and would either have to take what they were offered or leave it.

The company is known for having gone to dangerous measures to protect the monopoly. In Lily Allen's well known pop song, *The Fear*, she says ironically, "I want lots of clothes and fuck loads of diamonds. I hear people die while they're trying to find them." Indeed, De Beers's founder, Cecil Rhodes, is known for two things: for the Rhodes scholarship, and for his association with Apartheid in South Africa and the blood diamond controversy.

"In Sierra Leone a group known as the Revolutionary United Front killed, threatened, and even cut off the arms of people living and working in diamond villages until they were able to take control of the mines in the area. Then the group moved on to the next village to do more of the same, effectively terrorizing the entirety of Sierra Leone, to the point that many people fled their homes in fear. All in all, roughly 20,000 innocent people suffered bodily mutilation, 75,000 were killed and 2 million fled Sierra Leone altogether" (PBS Online Newshour, 2003).

De Beers is, perhaps, the best known for its marketing campaign that made every American woman believe that diamonds are forever and are synonymous with love, which, in light of all of the controversy and bloodshed associated with them, is ironic at best.

Walmart: Cult or Corporation?

Just about everyone has heard about the Walmart cheer that kicks off the store's morning work shift with a boisterous round of chanting, and if you haven't you can type "Walmart cheer" into Google and come up with several examples with no difficulty. This cheer reinforces the rigorous new recruit training, which teaches loyalty to the "Walmart way." A visit to the testimonials page of the website shows Walmart employees who describe how much better their life is now that they are part of the Walmart family. This is vaguely reminiscent of some of the cult practices mentioned in chapter five, and Walmart is not the only corporation to deliberately train employees to feel this way.

A lot of corporations are encouraging their employees to adopt a more blurry line between self and work. For example, "Biotech firm Genetech will organize babysitters for its staff rather than have them take time off to stay at home with a sick child. Consulting firm Deloitte offers backup care for an elderly parent or grandparent. Human Resources philosophers have ditched the mantra 'work life balance' for the more sinister (and employer friendly) 'work life integration'" (Whippman, 2012).

    Some corporations are taking on more power in the lives of their individual employees and making it convenience for them to accept that work is the most important aspect of their lives and that it should come before family obligations and before a social life. The principles that many corporate leaders preach can certainly be considered a form of brainwashing. As employees are told the same message over and over, as they hear it from their coworkers, as the logic of the management seeps into their minds and hearts, it becomes the truth. It becomes something that just is. All of the arguments that try to push it down have been dismissed. Your daughter might have a soccer game tonight, but she wouldn't even be able to play soccer if it weren't for the fact that you have this cushy job to pay for her registration fees and shoes and uniforms.

When you work for a corporation that demands everything from you, you may start to feel like the corporation is your real life and that everything outside of the corporation is less important than you had originally thought. Corporate leaders don't just demand your presence from nine to five for five days out of the week; they command your emotions, and, with them, your security, your times, and your devotion.

Whippman goes on to say that the cult-like devotion that so many corporations are demanding of their employees these days gives employers a lot more power over employees. They can demand more from their employees and treat them worse with far fewer consequences than they could have a decade ago. An employee might be asked to take on a special project, work later than before, and not get paid for it. What's more is that many times, the employee is happy to take on the extra work despite the fact that they aren't getting paid.

Why? Well, it's simple. They believe that they are getting some emotional worth from taking on more work in order to benefit the company—to benefit the family.

The Customer is Always Right...So Why is the Associate Always Grumpy?

The service sector is the fastest growing sector in North America, and with this growth has sprung the mentality that the customer is always right. This ideology is meant to portray goodwill toward the customer, making her feel that her needs are an associate's top priority and inspiring her to make more purchases.

But instead of forging an amicable relationship between a customer and the customer service personnel, it has succeeded in inspiring quite the opposite mentality. It sends customers the idea that they are entitled to the best service no matter who was waiting in line before them or how rude they are, while it sends associates the message that their managers aren't there to back them up but to criticize them and to undervalue the complicated public relations battle they play all day long with customers on the service floor.

As a result, the service sector seems to be in the business of manufacturing false cheer and resentment. Rather than creating an outpouring of goodwill toward customers, the mentality that the customer is always right creates a bigger separation between associates and management...and customers. Associates forced to adopt this mentality often develop resentment towards customers, especially in light of low pay and the customer's subsequent mentality of entitlement.

Adding to the sticky pot of drama, some corporations, Taco Bell, for example, require their employees to use specific greetings or scripts when addressing customers and attempting to sell items. Rather than promoting friendliness, this makes everything rote. The associate has to say it, but he doesn't have to mean it. The customer knows that it's a required speech and that knowledge serves to nullify it; the customer might either ignore it or make the assumption that the associate saying it doesn't mean it. In either case, it creates a disconnection between the customer and the associate that can inhibit a genuine feeling of goodwill toward each other.

Combined with the fact that a slow economy means that spending money for people is an emotional experience, and therefore not something that they very often do capriciously, industries like retail especially have seen a conflict between the way corporate management thinks things should be run and the ways in which customers respond to the associates. For example, at bookstore chain, Barnes & Noble, an associate is required to take the customer to a book and put it in their hand. They are additionally expected to tell the customer about the various membership programs for the purpose of getting them to pay the fee to sign up, increasing employees membership conversion rates, and satisfying the corporate agenda that proclaims that an employee is worthwhile only insofar as there is proof that they are selling the membership program.

In a slow economy, spending money on a membership that will encourage them to shop at Barnes & Noble more isn't necessarily in the budget. They decline. An associate, fearing losing their job will press the issue a little further. They will still get a no, but now the customer feels put upon and less likely to return anytime soon. The upper management plan is failing, but they are not there at the individual associate's level seeing that it is not for lack of trying. They draw the conclusion that employees aren't working hard enough and raise the membership conversion goals.

Forget about selling books. Forget about regional differences in customer temperament that account for the different ways of saying now (in Minnesota, a customer's "Thanks for letting me know" is usually a no. In New York it's not a no until it's a "No"). Corporate wants the numbers that prove that customers are loyal to the company. They don't have numbers for how many times a Barnes & Noble customer says, "I'll get it on Amazon" when they are pressed for cash and an associate is pressed to upsell a program on top of the product. They want numbers to prove that their customers will come back and keep buying from them, and this is the best they can think of. Instead of focusing on selling more books, it seems like they've gotten lost in trying to measure worth based on something that does a poor job of measuring worth to begin with.

How to Unbrainwash From Corporate Ideologies

The purpose of the corporation is to make you practice unwavering loyalty by giving them your money. Sure, they also want to bring you stuff that you want, but mostly they want you to buy stuff whether you need or want it or not. If you've ever impulsively bought something without understanding quite why you did so, these unbrainwashing techniques are for you.

For starters, pay attention to the language that corporations use to persuade you of something. Are they telling it like it is or have they reframed it? Is your expenditure an investment? Are they claiming that you have to spend money to save it? Is the loyalty program that they're advertising called a rewards program? You don't have to blindly accept the positive reframing without thinking about what it's saying underneath all of the nice sounding words. Most corporations, whether you're working for them or buying from them, will have a way of wording potentially costly or in some other way negative things so that you perceive it in a positive light. Budget and staff cuts are called downsizing. Laying off employees is called opening doors for opportunity.

Especially when it comes to large purchases, research the products and services you are thinking about investing in. Use multiple sources to educate yourself about your options. You don't have to just stick with the information presented on the car dealership's website. If you think you might be interested in purchasing a GM vehicle, talk with your friends who own GM vehicles. Find out what they like and don't like about it. Ask them which dealership they bought their vehicle from and whether the staff there seemed trustworthy.

Not all locations are created equal. Do some shopping around and see which locations seem the most forthcoming with their information. You're looking for a location with associates and managers who answer your questions clearly and directly while treating you and your potential business with respect, regardless of what you look like or the quality of vehicle you drove up to the lot in.

When you enter a sales floor, you should be cognizant of the scripts at play, and always remember to treat people like humans. A basic human rule is that if you treat people as if they have inherent worth and dignity, they will be most likely to treat you the same way—and give you excellent service. People in the service industry are sometimes treated in an uppity manner by entitled customers simply because of the assumption that they must not be smart enough to be working in a cubicle instead, an assumption which is simply not true. A lot of intelligent people work in the service industry simply because they like to serve people, despite all of the rude customers who make their jobs difficult as well as the propaganda coming from corporate headquarters.

Remember a service worker's humanity. Look them in the eye. Understand that they might be pushing you to sign up for a rewards program because their managers are breathing down their neck about it, not because they don't know how to read nonverbal cues. For all you know, their manager is standing the next row down listening to them and critiquing how they're doing with their sales pitch. You don't have to let this influence whether you give in, but being a good person to them and not making them feel like a jerk for doing their job is always a good way to handle the situation. Keeping all of this in mind when shopping or eating out will not only get you better service overall, but it will help you avoid the brainwashed assumptions about the people serving you.

Compare competing brands. If you feel drawn to one brand over another, ask yourself why that is. Is it simply because one brand has a more attractive advertising campaign? Or are there specific qualities that objectively make one better than the other? If the items you are comparing are inexpensive, you might buy them both in order to compare and form an opinion. Especially if the item in question is a food item, check the labels. Some brands of raisins are more expensive, but, to be honest, a raisin is still a raisin, whether it's in the more expensive bright red box or the off brand white box. Many products are like this—essentially the same regardless of the brand—yet we still will buy the more expensive version simply because we are familiar with the label. As a general rule of thumb, if the item in question is something that doesn't require a recipe to create (packaged fruits and vegetables, spices, rice, etc.), then there's probably little, if any, difference between the several different versions of a product on the shelf.

Come up with ways that support small businesses rather than the corporate entities. It comes as no surprise that corporate giants like Walmart, Target, Amazon, and Sears shamelessly put privately owned local businesses out of business. They can order greater quantities of an item and sell it for a cheaper price, effectively driving smaller competition out of business. It's easy to be swayed by the cheapness of a product alone and assume that where you're getting it from doesn't matter a lot. That's what they want you to think. But long term, it's important to also think about the future of your community. Where you shop can have a huge impact on your local infrastructure.

If you are working for a corporation that demands a lot of you in terms of your personal life it's important that you think through the implications of this. Set some boundaries for yourself and enforce them. Despite what upper corporate management will try to make you believe, the company can't satisfy all of your needs, and it should not be expecting you to habitually sacrifice your needs and wellbeing for the good of the company. The company is not your family; your family is your family, and a large corporation that insists on being thought of as a family is probably trying to manipulate you into giving more of yourself for less. If it comes down to it, decide if this is a company that is worth working for if they're going to take such a large part of your life. Sometimes it will be worth it for you; sometimes it won't.

"We sell for less" should not become your personal mantra.

CONCLUSION: TRUTH, LIES, AND A CULTURE OF PARANOIA

As I stand in the night looking out over a city of lights, noise, and tall building silhouettes scraping the clear, violet-orange sky, it's too easy to envision the rampant criminal activity that is probably going on at this very moment as any place along the quiet residential block. Every noise is a footstep; every wisp of breeze is a breath on my neck.

A car passes behind me. Did it slow down as it passed me, or did I imagine that? A loud laugh erupts from somewhere upriver and chills my spine. It's not a wild animal, I tell myself, because that would be crazy. This is the city.

Anyone could be out there waiting for me to blink for a moment, to let my guard down. I watch a figure across the bridge from where I'm standing pause for a moment as he walks, and I wonder if he's the one—the violent criminal who could send me into the river below my feet. He walks toward me, then away. Nothing happens. I don't expect it to, yet I can't shake the feeling that my time is coming, and it's just as likely to be now as it is to be later.

I lean against the cool railing once again. Every violent news story I've seen in the past week does another quick round through my head. It's like a security man on patrol—in my own head. I'm being ridiculous, and I know it. After all, the crime rate in this neighborhood is low for a city, and most of it is traffic violations and speeding tickets. The probability that anything horrible and tragic is going to happen to me is actually pretty low, all things considered.

Then again, I remember that adage that some friend told me back in middle school. Something about how your chances of getting hit by lightning increase when you go outside in a storm, stand under a tree, shake your fist in the air, and say, "Storms suck!" I immediately remembered a video a friend had showed me on Youtube last week. A man had been struck by lightning twice in a row. I wondered if he had lived. I guessed so. It would be in pretty bad taste to post a video of some guy getting struck by lightning if you ran over afterwards and discovered that he hadn't lived to tell about it. Then again, people can come up with some weird justifications for things.

I shook my head and turned to walk home, realizing that I'd spent several minutes on a perfectly clear, cool night staring at the view of the city skyline without really seeing it. What was wrong with me?

With all this talk about brainwashing and mind control and the thousands of conspiracy theories out there (and the occasional few that have been proven to be true), it's easy to fall victim to a culture of paranoia. It seems like everyone around you is out for their own gain and out to manipulate you to their ends. Everyone seems to have their own un-falsifiable rumor to proliferate. Every political, religious, educational, and corporate entity seems to be after your hard earned money and your soul.

    Take a deep breath. Yes, it is true that the world is big, and yes, it's full of people who don't care about you. Sometimes businesses are scams, and sometimes corporations are out to rob you of your life outside of them. Sometimes it seems like everyone has a reason to abuse, manipulate, and cheat you out of something that is rightfully yours. Sometimes it's hard to know what's right, what's real, and what is straight up brainwashing. But the upside is that most of people aren't specifically out to get *you*. Resisting brainwashing, mind control, and manipulation might not always be an easy time, but the principles that you must follow in order to keep to the truths are fairly straightforward. If you show up for your life every day, that's the first step. If you learn to listen actively and engage in your surroundings, rather than passively accepting things no matter what, then you will put yourself at a distinct advantage over those who act without thinking or those who don't act at all until they are told what to do.

We are more than robots. We have the ability to think about things in ways that no animal on earth can. We have the ability to act on our beliefs. And we have the ability to learn from the beliefs and actions of others. With minds like these, who needs passivity?

Why Does Our Culture Hate Proselytizing?

Coinciding with a rise in the belief that tolerance is the key to attaining world peace, is the belief that proselytizing is not only annoying and difficult, but it is also morally reprehensible. With the word come images of soapbox street preachers shouting at the top of their voices, "Repent, sinners! The kingdom of God is at hand, and you're all going to hell!" Or maybe you're thinking back on all of the brainwashing cults out there whose members stare into your eyes, say a few key persuasive phrases, and convert you to some freaky cult religion on the spot.

Proselytizing, our culture tells us, goes hand in hand with intolerance, and one of the greatest insults of our day is to be thought intolerant. Why do we feel this way? Certainly intolerance is not always bad. Yet, liberal (not to be confused with Democratic) culture disagrees there too, declaring that all ideas are equal, all truths are relative, and anyone who says otherwise should have their opinion snuffed out.

If worldwide tolerance will lead to peace, it will, undoubtedly lead to peace with the wrong entities. After all, it is not the poor, the sick, and the marginalized who have the power to keep the peace. It is not those suffering the consequences of unjust wars who have the power to keep the peace. It is the oppressors who have the resources to keep the poor destitute and the marginalized on the margins; it is the oppressors who have the clout to threaten our peace should we object to what they're doing.

Tolerance of corporate entities that exploit sweatshop laborers in Bangladesh so that Americans can wear cheap cotton tee shirts won't bring justice to the exploited; it will perpetuate injustice. In cases like this, what has tolerance solved? Is saving a few dollars at Walmart worth the diminished quality of life of a child overseas?

This is the object of proselytizing. Proselytizing is what keeps people informed and thoughtful.

The definition of proselytizing according to dictionary.com is to attempt to convert someone to an idea, a belief, or a faith. It's an attempt to be overtly persuasive in order to win someone to your own perspective. It's the opposite of how our culture defines tolerance, which is a passive acceptance of all ideas and beliefs.

We live by a double standard in our society; marketers spend all day every day hundreds of times per moment trying to persuade us to buy products and services and vote for certain political agendas, and they do it without our realizing it and much of the time without our consent, but if another person attempts to overtly persuade us to believe in what they believe, we get offended, call them narrow-minded bigots, and staunchly close our ears. After all, what if they brainwash us?

But let me remind you that there is a world of difference between listening to someone while they explain their perspective to you and letting someone brainwash you. The fact that someone is trying to persuade us of something is not always indicative of a need to assert their control and be right; but the fact that we are shutting them up by telling them not to foist their ideas upon us is definitely indicative of that very thing.

A need to feel in control of our lives in a world filled with chaos causes us to close ourselves off to persuasion and public discourse in order to maintain that sense of control, but the tradeoff is that, as a result, we leave our beliefs largely uninspected and susceptible to derailment should an actual manipulative person or organization happen upon us. In order to brainwash, an institution must apply stress and shake our confidence in our worldview and set of beliefs. This is much easier for them to accomplish if we don't know why we believe what we believe, because we've never thought it out or allowed ourselves or anyone else to challenge it.

Allowing people to explain their opinions to us and challenge our own provides an opportunity for us to explore questions we might not have thought of on our own. It fleshes out our faith, so to speak. When done in a respectful setting, proselytizing allows the sharing of ideas. It's a social contract, of sorts. Both the one attempting to persuade and the one being persuaded are opening themselves up to questions and scrutiny of their beliefs. Respectful persuasion is a two way street.

Tolerance sounds nice on the surface, and perhaps it was a well-intentioned idea when people first started flinging the word around. As call for mutual respect and love, it's an excellent aim for society, but at this time, that's no longer what the word stands for. Tolerance is a trump card thrown down to suppress an idea that seems too radical or critical of something or someone in our society. It's become a way of saying to each other, "You believe what you believe, and I'll believe what I believe. Your experience doesn't mean anything to me, and mine doesn't have to mean anything to you. We have nothing of value to speak into each others' lives."

Tolerance has stripped us of our right, or perhaps our obligation, to speak into another person's life. Instead of challenging our neighbors when we believe that they are hurting or abusing someone, we think, "Well, that's not how I would treat my wife, but I guess that's just how he views marriage. Who am I to tell him that his opinion is wrong?" The idea of tolerance takes away the pangs of conscience that come from staying silent when we disagree. It takes away our care for our fellow humans and replaces it with indifference. If we care about a person, do we stand by and watch her destroy herself without first trying to persuade her to take a different course?

Our paranoia about having our beliefs challenged and falling prey to brainwashing, mind control, negative influence, and manipulation is understandable, but it's not an excuse for indifference and lack of engagement in the lives of the people around us.

Engage in Well-Measured Risks

When I say to engage in risks, I don't mean that you should act recklessly and do things that are unwise in the name of taking risks. To be sure, not all risks are worthwhile risks to be taking, and it's important that you be able to differentiate between good ones and bad ones. Going alone with a group of religious fanatics to a house in the desert because they've promised that you will achieve enlightenment is not a well-measured risk. A well-measured risk is one that is likely to bring you success or some kind of positive personal development even if you fail. A well-measured risk doesn't have to be realistic, necessarily. For example, writing a novel in a month as many people do in the month of November during National Novel Writing Month. But participants go into it understanding what it's about, what their goals are, and (the successful ones, anyway) which a realistic plan of attack.

A well-measured risk means engaging in the world in a way that is new to you.

What does healthy engagement with society look like? This entire book has cast dubious light on many of the institutions that fill our daily lives. Your children and significant other may try to use your emotions against you. Your political party may try to pull the wool over your eyes. Your religion might say one thing and do the opposite. Your social media might promise you a lifetime of social connection and togetherness and then deliver on hours of time spent alone at your computer. Your technology might lure you in with promises of freedom and then chain you to itself more rigidly than you were ever chained to anything before.

I'm saying that all of the systems that we've set up for ourselves can control us as easily as they can free us, but we should not be running away from them in terror. The systems are no better or worse or smarter or dumber than the people who created them and run them. Checking out is a recipe for disaster not a solution to avoid brainwashing.

Join in with the world. Participate in life. But do so with a healthy respect for others. Do so while continually striving to understand people and human nature better than you had before. Don't forget to see people as people, not as objects or as annoyances or inconveniences. Participate in the political rally. Start the new relationship. Go to college. Be active in your church. Serve your country. Shop at Target. But don't do so blindly.

Life is nothing but a series of risks. Everything is a risk. Getting up and leaving your warm bed in the morning is a risk. Applying for a job is a risk. Saying hi to an attractive stranger on the bus is a risk. Signing up for a club is a risk. Donating time or money is a risk. Thinking and talking about religion is a risk. Planting a garden is a risk. Eating a cheeseburger is a risk. Even standing on a bridge over the river staring at the city skyline in a perfectly safe neighborhood is a risk. The amount of media we consume only feeds our sensitivity to the fact that everything we do can be a risky business. Staying alive is a pretty risky business.

Your goal should be to look for the risks that you feel are worth it for you to take—even when you know that you might fail. Especially when you know that you might fail. The decisions that are most worth making are often the scariest to make. You'll have the most to lose. Weigh your options. Test your ideas. Ask for advice. Do research.

Spontaneously go for a walk in the city at night, for heaven's sake, but do so intelligently, and do so consciously. Each moment only comes once. If you squander that moment with worry about things you have little control over, you don't get it back. You don't get a do over. There's not Command Z button to undo time so that you can try again and get it right this time. This can be debilitating, but it shouldn't be. If you don't ever take any risks, you'll have no basis for learning how to improve yourself and get to where you want to be in life.

Taking risks is active and requires a sense of intentionality. When you live your life with intention and thoughtfulness, you are strengthening your neural connections and giving your mind the best protection it can get from brainwashing, mind control, controlling people, manipulation, and propaganda.

BIBLIOGRAPHY

Aesthetic realism is a cult. (n.d.). Retrieved July 2, 2015, from http://michaelbluejay.com/x/

Akin, J. (n.d.). Is Atheism a Religion? Retrieved July 2, 2015, from http://www.strangenotions.com/is-atheism-a-religion/

Allen, M. (2015, May 27). Failed scary predictions that never came true in the USA. Retrieved July 1, 2015, from http://www.truthin7minutes.com/failed-predictions/

Anderson, D. (2005). Television and Very Young Children. *American Behavioral Scientist*, 505-522.

Andersen, S., & Zimbardo, P. (1980, November 1). How to Resist Mind Control. Retrieved July 2, 2015, from http://exitsupportnetwork.com/artcls/mindctrl/resist.htm

Anderson, R. (1999, December 11). The Millennium Bug - Reasons Not To Panic. Retrieved July 1, 2015, from http://www.cl.cam.ac.uk/~rja14/Papers/y2k.pdf

Babies and Toddlers Should Learn from Play Not Screens. (2011, October 18). Retrieved July 1, 2015, from https://www.aap.org/en-us/about-the-aap/aap-press-room/pages/Babies-and-Toddlers-Should-Learn-from-Play-Not-Screens.aspx

Behar, R. (1991, March 6). Scientology: The Thriving Cult of Greed and Power. Retrieved July 2, 2015, from https://www.cs.cmu.edu/~dst/Fishman/time-behar.html

Beware of Land Sharks. (2001, September 7). Retrieved July 1, 2015, from http://www.cbsnews.com/news/beware-of-land-sharks/

Britt, R. (2007, December 20). 7 Medical Myths Even Doctors Believe. Retrieved July 3, 2015

CG, B. (n.d.). Decision Neuroscience. Retrieved July 1, 2015, from http://brettcg.tumblr.com/DecisionNeuroscience

Charman-Anderson, S. (2012, August 28). Fake Reviews: Amazon's Rotten Core. Retrieved July 1, 2015, from http://www.forbes.com/sites/suwcharmananderson/2012/08/28/fake-reviews-amazons-rotten-core/

Coates, J. (2000, April 17). Overblown Or Not, Y2k Scare Awakened Amrica's Sleeping Giants. Retrieved July 1, 2015, from http://articles.chicagotribune.com/2000-04-17/business/0004180371_1_web-sites-egghead-com-business-to-business-e-commerce

Coopersmith, N. (2000, January 22). 4 Misconceptions Jews Have About Judaism. Retrieved July 3, 2015, from http://www.aish.com/jl/p/ph/48971136.html

Covino, G. (Ed.). (2005, November 16). 'My Lobotomy': Howard Dully's Journey. Retrieved July 1, 2015, from http://www.npr.org/2005/11/16/5014080/my-lobotomy-howard-dullys-journey

Denmark's Tvind. (2002, March 21). Retrieved July 2, 2015, from http://news.bbc.co.uk/2/hi/programmes/crossing_continents/1885116.stm

Dubner, S. (2012, February 16). How Biased Is Your Media?: A New Freakonomics Radio Podcast. Retrieved July 1, 2015, from http://freakonomics.com/2012/02/16/how-biased-is-your-media/

The Economics of Y2K and the Impact on the United States. (1999, November 17).

Retrieved July 1, 2015, from http://www.esa.doc.gov/sites/default/files/y2k_1.pdf

Elshtain, J. B. (2008). Toleration, proselytizing, and the politics of recognition. In T. Banchoff (Ed.), *Religious pluralism, globalization, and world politics* (pp. 89-104). Oxford: Oxford University Press.

Engel, B. (2008). *The nice girl syndrome stop being manipulated and abused--and start standing up for yourself.* Hoboken, NJ: John Wiley & Sons.

Ewing, K. (2008, January 12). Beijing Hotels. Retrieved July 2, 2015, from http://www.atimes.com/atimes/China/JA12Ad01.html

Evans, P., & Jones, S. (2013, January 22). Is Atheism A Religion? Retrieved July 3, 2015, from http://www.nytimes.com/roomfordebate/2013/01/22/is-atheism-a-religion/at-

atheist-church-in-london-no-faith-required

Finger, S. (1994). *Origins of neuroscience: A history of explorations into brain function*. New York: Oxford University Press.

Fleischacker, S. (2011, October 13). Mormonism: Cult vs. religion: What's the difference? Retrieved July 2, 2015, from http://articles.baltimoresun.com/2011-10-13/news/bs-ed-mormons-20111013_1_cult-religion-mormonism

Foster, N. (2014, December 18). The Show That Replaced Firefly: Fastlane. Retrieved July 1, 2015, from http://blog.platypustv.com/?p=105

Frase, L., & Streshly, W. (2000). *Top ten myths in education: Fantasies Americans love to believe*. Lanham, MD: Scarecrow Press.

Gehrtz, J. (2011, January 23). Bad Eromance Kindles Love of Fighting Fraud. Retrieved

July 1, 2015, from http://romancescams.org/media/20110118--StarTribuneMN.pdf

Grant, A. (2014, January 2). The Dark Side of Emotional Intelligence. Retrieved July 1, 2015, from http://www.theatlantic.com/health/archive/2014/01/the-dark-side-of-emotional-intelligence/282720/

Graves, P. (2010). *Consumer.ology the market research myth, the truth about consumers and the psychology of shopping*. Boston: Nicholas Brealey Publishing.

Griffin, E. (2012). *A first look at communication theory* (8th ed.). New York, New York: McGraw-Hill.

Haan, T. (2012, January 30). Basic Training Explained. Retrieved July 1, 2015, from http://thewisesloth.com/2012/01/30/trainee-moon-goes-to-basic-training/

Hale, J. (2011, April 18). Understanding Research Methodology 4: Peer Review Process. Retrieved July 1, 2015, from http://psychcentral.com/blog/archives/2011/04/18/understanding-research-methodology-4-peer-review-process/

Harrison, K. (2003). Television viewers' ideal body proportions: The case of the curvaceously thin woman. Sex Roles, 48, 255-264.

Hassam. (n.d.). Government technology to read your thoughts and implant new ones. Retrieved on July 2, 2015, from http://www.jeffpolachek.com/mind-control/mc-research-docs/199-government-technology-to-read-your-thoughts-and-implant-new-ones

Hedges, C. (2009). *Empire of illusion: The end of literacy and the triumph of spectacle.* New York: Nation Books.

Hoyt, Alia. (2008, April 21). How the African

Diamond Trade Works. HowStuffWorks.com. <http://money.howstuffworks.com/african-diamond-trade.htm> 02 July 2015.

ISCA. (n.d.). Retrieved July 3, 2015, from http://islamicsupremecouncil.org/understanding-islam/legal-rulings/5-jihad-a-misunderstood-concept-from-islam.html?start=9

Keeping kids connected: How Schools and Teachers Can Help All Students Feel Good About School . . . and Why That Matters. (2000). Retrieved July 2, 2015.

Kilbourne, J. (1999). *Deadly persuasion: Why women and girls must fight the addictive power of advertising.* New York, NY: Free Press.

Layton, J. (n.d.). How Brainwashing Works. Retrieved July 1, 2015, from http://science.howstuffworks.com/life/inside-the-mind/human-brain/brainwashing1.htm

Levine, M. P., & Harrison, K. (2009). Effects of media on eating disorders and body image. In J. Bryant & M. B. Oliver (Eds.), *Media effects: Advances in theory and research* (3rd ed., pp. 490–515). New York: Routledge.

Levin, D., & Rosenquest, B. (2001). The Increasing Role of Electronic Toys in the Lives of Infants and Toddlers: Should we be concerned? *Ciec Contemporary Issues in Early Childhood,* 242-242.

Levitt, S., & Dubner, S. (2005). *Freakonomics: A rogue economist explores the hidden side of everything.* New York: William Morrow.

Lindstrom, M. (2011). *Brandwashed: Tricks companies use to manipulate our minds and persuade us to buy.* New York: Crown Business.

Marlowe, D. (1987, May 22). Statistics Can

Support Any Point -- And I Have Numbers To Prove That. Retrieved July 2, 2015, from http://articles.orlandosentinel.com/1987-05-22/business/0130160247_1_people-use-statistics-statistics-to-prove-deceptive-statistics

Marshall, S. (2004). *True lies*. New York: Plume.

Martino, J. (2012, December 5). How hemp became illegal: the marijuana link. Retrived on July 2, 2015, from http://www.collective-evolution.com/2012/12/05/how-hemp-became-illegal-the-marijuana-link/

McDermott, D. (n.d.). Stop mind control - How to spot it. Retrieved July 1, 2015, from http://www.decision-making-confidence.com/stop-mind-control.html

Mehta, D. (n.d.). Brain Washing Concepts for Hindus. Retrieved July 2, 2015, from http://hmsamerica.org/opinion/dilip-mehta/brain-washing-concepts-for-hindus

Meltzer, T. (2011, May 16). Planking: A brief history. Retrieved July 1, 2015, from http://www.theguardian.com/world/2011/may/16/planking-a-brief-history

Miller, D. (2004). Searching for god knows what. Nashville, TN: Thomas Nelson, Inc.

Ni, P. (2014, June 1). How to Spot and Stop Manipulators. Retrieved July 1, 2015, from https://www.psychologytoday.com/blog/communication-success/201406/how-spot-and-stop-manipulators

Oremus, W. (2015, June 22). Amazon Will Start Paying Some E-Book Authors by "Pages Read." That's Smarter Than It Sounds. . Retrieved July 1, 2015, from http://www.slate.com/blogs/future_tense/2015/06/22/amazon_e_book_author_royalties_why_paying_by_pages_read_ makes_sense.html

Pappas, S. (2011, February 28). Psy-Ops: Military Experts Say It's Not 'Brainwashing' Retrieved July 1, 2015, from http://www.livescience.com/12987-psy-ops-brainwashing.html

Patrick, T., & Dulack, T. (1976). *Let our children go!* New York: Dutton.

Penny, L. (2005). *Your call is important to us: The truth about bullshit.* New York: Crown.

Postman, N. (2006). *Amusing ourselves to death: Public discourse in the age of show business* (20th anniversary ed.). New York, N.Y., U.S.A.: Penguin Books.

Powell, G. (2012). Danish studies suggesting low and moderate prenatal alcohol exposure has no adverse effects on children aged 5 years did not use appropriate or effective measures of executive functioning. *BJOG: An International Journal of Obstetrics &*

Gynaecology, 1669-1670.

Rape and Sexual Abuse Survivors Message Board and Chat Room - After Silence - Rape -. (n.d.). Retrieved July 1, 2015, from http://www.aftersilence.org/rape.php

The rise & fall of the prefrontal lobotomy. (2007, July 24). Retrieved July 1, 2015, from http://scienceblogs.com/neurophilosophy/2007/07/24/inventing-the-lobotomy/

Roark, C. (2015, June 30). If You Changed Your Facebook Pic to a Rainbow Flag, You May Have Fallen Into One BIG Trap. Retrieved July 1, 2015, from http://capitalismisfreedom.com/rainbow-flag-facebook/

Rudder, C. (2014). *Dataclysm: Who we are when we think no one's looking.* Crown.

Schettini, S. (2012, September 30). When Buddhism is a Cult. Retrieved July 2, 2015.

Schor, J. (2004). *Born to buy: The commercialized child and the new consumer culture.* New York: Scribner.

Shapiro, B. (2004). *Brainwashed: How universities indoctrinate America's youth.* Nashville: WND Books.

Shermer, M. (2010, November 17). The Conspiracy Theory Detector. Retrieved July 3, 2015, from http://www.scientificamerican.com/article/the-conspiracy-theory-director/

Simpson, E. (2015, March 2). Why We Failed to Win a Decisive Victory in Afghanistan. Retrieved July 3, 2015.

Smith, A., & Anderson, M. (2015, April 20). 5 facts about online dating. Retrieved July 1, 2015, from http://www.pewresearch.org/fact-tank/2015/04/20/5-facts-about-online-dating/

Stiles, C. (2014, November 18). Five Hoaxes

You'd Never Fall for in a Million Years ... or would you? Retrieved July 1, 2015, from http://blog.grantham.edu/online-hoaxes-not-accredited-online-degree-program

Thomas, S. (2007). *Buy, buy baby: How consumer culture manipulates parents and harms young minds.* Boston: Houghton Mifflin.

Thompson, D. (2010, July 28). Islam may not be a cult, but cult-like Islam is flourishing – Telegraph Blogs. Retrieved July 2, 2015, from http://blogs.telegraph.co.uk/news/damianthompson/100048923/islam-may-not-be-a-cult-but-cult-like-islam-is-flourishing/

"Truth and Justice." PBS Online Newshour. Jan. 23, 2003. http://www.pbs.org/newshour/bb/africa/jan-june03/truth_&_justice_1-23.html

Urbanski, D. (2014, November 1). How Many New Ebola Cases in U.S. by End of 2014? Experts Weigh In. Retrieved July 3, 2015.

Weiner, D. (2002). *Power freaks: Dealing with them in the workplace or anyplace.* Amherst, NY: Prometheus Books.

Weiner, T. (2008, July 5). Remembering Brainwashing. Retrieved July 3, 2015.

What is internet censorship? (n.d.). Retrieved July 1, 2015, from http://www.huffingtonpost.com/ruth-whippman/how-corporate-america-is-_b_2171040.htmlhttp://www.amnesty.org.au/china/comments/10926/

Whippman, R. (2012, November 24). How corporate America is turning into a cult and why it's harming the American employee. Retrieved July 2, 2015, from

Wilson, L. (2014, February 1). Bainwashing. Retrieved July 1, 2015, from http://drlwilson.com/articles/BRAINWA

SH.htm

Wong, D. (2008, September 23). 6 Brainwashing Techniques They're Using On You Right Now. Retrieved July 1, 2015, from http://www.cracked.com/article_16656_6-brainwashing-techniques-theyre-using-you-right-now_p2.html

Zhao, E. (2012, April 2). Elementary School Arts Classes Reduced, Report Says. Retrieved July 2, 2015, from http://www.huffingtonpost.com/2012/04/02/report-arts-classes-at-el_n_1398550.html

Zimnisky, P. (2013, April 9). Diamonds: Driven by market forces for the first time in 100 years. Retrieved July 2, 2015, from http://www.resourceinvestor.com/2013/04/09/diamonds-driven-market-forces-first-time-100-years?page=2

Printed in France by Amazon
Brétigny-sur-Orge, FR